Library Use

Library Use

HANDBOOK FOR PSYCHOLOGY

THIRD EDITION

Jeffrey G. Reed and Pam M. Baxter

American Psychological Association, Washington, DC

Published by
American Psychological Association
750 First Street, NE
Washington, DC 20002
www.apa.org

To order
APA Order Department
P.O. Box 92984
Washington, DC 20090-2984

Tel: (800) 374-2721, Direct: (202) 336-5510
Fax: (202) 336-5502, TDD/TTY: (202) 336-6123
Online: www.apa.org/books/
E-mail: order@apa.org

In the U.K., Europe, Africa, and the Middle East, copies may be ordered from
American Psychological Association
3 Henrietta Street
Covent Garden, London
WC2E 8LU England

Typeset in Stone Serif by NOVA Graphic Services, Jamison, PA

Printer: Phoenix Color Corporation, Hagerstown, MD
Cover Designer: Michael Hentges Design, Alexandria, VA
Project Manager: NOVA Graphic Services, Jamison, PA

The opinions and statements published are the responsibility of the authors, and such opinions and statements do not necessarily represent the policies of the American Psychological Association.

Library of Congress Cataloging-in-Publication Data
Reed, Jeffrey G., 1948-
  Library use : handbook for psychology / by Jeffrey G. Reed and Pam M. Baxter.— 3rd ed.
    p. cm.
Includes bibliographical references and index.
  ISBN 1-55798-992-3 (alk. paper)
  1. Psychological literature. 2. Psychology—Library resources. 3. Psychology—Research. I. Baxter, Pam M., 1955- II. Title.
BF76.8.R43 2003
025.5'6'02415—dc21   2002043753

British Library Cataloguing-in-Publication Data
A CIP record is available from the British Library.

Printed in the United States of America
First Edition

Contents

110197

Preface

In writing this new edition, we have completely updated the contents of *Library Use: Handbook for Psychology*. We have added much information but have retained the features people found most useful in earlier editions.

Significant changes in information publishing and distribution have taken place over the past decade. Many new resources are available. Library catalogs, many periodical indexes and abstracts, and other sources once available only in printed form can now be accessed electronically in an increasing number of libraries. In addition, the Internet and World Wide Web have emerged as a significant vehicle for information access and delivery. For this reason, we have focused extensively on use of electronic media and have reduced emphasis on use of hard-copy print resources.

Chapter search topic examples in the second edition were evaluated, and many were replaced. Topics that were retained have been updated and include new references and sources. To ensure that readers have some familiarity with each sample topic, summaries have been provided to introduce the topic; in some cases, summaries are slightly longer than in the second edition. Recognizing the breadth of the field of psychology, we selected topics from many areas and tried to balance the book by including subject matter in both applied and theoretical areas. In each case, we attempted to find topics that would

- appeal to the interests of many students,
- represent some aspect of contemporary psychology,
- generally not require highly technical knowledge,
- have a body of published literature, and
- be available in a typical college library.

We expanded the chapter on computer searching. Its appearance earlier in the book highlights the fact that computer searching principles are used in several subsequent chapters. We also added coverage of the World Wide Web to chapter 11. Many new services have appeared, including Ask ERIC, PubMed, and GPO Access. The world of information technology is changing so rapidly that what appears on your monitor one day may be different from what you see the next. During the time that we were preparing the third edition, we encountered many changes in reference sources. In addition, some services are available from a variety of vendors who offer different front-end user interfaces. As in the first and second editions, we rely heavily on figures to illustrate the use of sources. All figures in this edition are new. We have attempted to make figures as generic as possible in recognition of both vendor differences and the changing nature of information technology.

We hope that these and other changes make this book useful as you enter this world of information.

Acknowledgments

As with prior editions, many people assisted us in the development of the third edition of *Library Use: Handbook for Psychology*.

We are especially indebted to the people who helped by providing ideas for chapter examples, who reviewed portions of the manuscript, and who reviewed the entire manuscript. These include Suzette Astley, Ruth Ault, Anne Buchanan, Karen Duffy, Michelle Majewski, Margaret Matlin, Amy McCabe, Jon Nicoud, Julia Stiles, Martha Wilding, and Joan Zook.

Library staff at the following institutions supported our use of their facilities and collections: Cornell University, Lawrence University, Marian College of Fond du Lac, Ripon College, Silver Lake College, University of Wisconsin—Fond du Lac, University of Wisconsin—Milwaukee, and University of Wisconsin—Oshkosh.

Many people at the American Psychological Association (APA) have been very helpful with this project. Lansing Hays understood our transition from writing a book focused on print media to writing one emphasizing digital resources, while Emily Welsh guided us through editorial development and Robin Bonner managed the production process. Carolyn Gosling, Linda Beebe, and Marion Harrell provided information on new and evolving products and clarification about PsycINFO and other APA products.

Many people contributed to the development of the first and second editions of this book, which laid the foundation for this revision: Suzette Astley, Susan Bedford, Paddy Berson, Monica Brien, Brenda Bryant, Lawrence Casler, William Deeds, Arlene Dempsey, Daren Duffy, Ellen Dykes, Howard Egeth, K. Della Ferguson, Priscilla Geahigan, Carolyn Gosling, Richard Hudiburg, Robert Jordan, Donald Kausler, MaryAnn Lahey, Adelaide LaVerdi, Margaret Matlin, Kathleen McGowan, Jerry Meyer, Larry Murdock, Lynn Offerman, Paul Olczak, Virginia O'Leary, Mary Joan Parise, David Parish, Richard Pringle, George Rebok, Lanna Ruddy, Mary Lynn Skutley, Harriet Sleggs, Nancy Smith, Charles Thurston, Gregory Trautt, and Raymond Wolfe.

We appreciate the continued support of our spouses, Sylvia and Gordon, throughout this project. To all of these people, and others unknown to us who helped, thanks for your support and assistance.

Library Use

1 Introduction: Getting Started

A LIBRARY is a storehouse of information. Observations, reflections, empirical data, theories, and so forth are continually reported in books, journals, and other forms by researchers in many fields. You will examine some of this knowledge in your formal education. A textbook chapter or two or several meeting sessions of a course will deal with a variety of important problems and issues, and some prominent topics may involve a whole course. But there is much information to which you will never be exposed in a classroom, and you will find that you must pursue some issues on your own. Your immediate need for information may stem from a research paper that you will have to write for which you must use the library.

We have found that most students have little formal training in how to use a library. Typically, a student's experience is limited to a superficial exposure to the online catalog, a periodical index, and the reserve desk to complete assigned class readings. Consequently, when confronted with a topic requiring use of more specialized tools, many students fail to locate the information needed.

Although faculty members generally recognize students' need to explore the psychological literature, many are hesitant to assume the task of teaching library use skills. Some faculty members have never had the benefit of such instruction themselves or assume that their students have "picked it up" in some other setting or class. Often, courses on research methods stress the conduct of empirical research and reporting, allowing little time for instruction in library use skills. Although some faculty tap the resources of the library's staff to teach such skills, these library sessions usually take only one classroom hour, seldom provide hands-on experience, and offer only a glimpse of the resources available. Thus *Library Use: Handbook for Psychology, Third Edition* was written to bridge the gap between the need that a student embarking on a psychology research project has for information and the information that is available from the college library.

THE AUDIENCE

This book is intended as an introduction to library research for college students, and it can supplement instruction in library research methods provided in the classroom setting. We anticipate that typical readers will be enrolled in a college course in experimental psychology or research methods or will be engaged in independent study. This book will also be useful to students in other situations involving research projects, such as honors papers, theses, and dissertations.

We have tried to identify a group of core resources that students would typically find in a small- to medium-sized college library generally serving a campus enrolling 1,000 to 5,000 students. In addition, the book briefly discusses specialized resources important to researchers in particular subfields of psychology and that can be found on campuses serving a larger student body or offering advanced degree work. Therefore, graduate students and faculty may find the information presented about some of the specialized sources to be a useful supplement to their knowledge of bibliographic tools.

SCOPE AND APPROACH

We have made few assumptions about a student's library knowledge and research skills. The book provides brief background information concerning each type of source discussed and presents a minisearch to illustrate the use of each major source. Numerous figures illustrate the principles and sources discussed. Throughout, we emphasize the process of selecting and narrowing a topic, identifying a few key resources, and using this information as a background to searching key tools to the literature.

Library Use: Handbook for Psychology will inform you about sources of information made available by college libraries, how these sources are organized, and how to use them. Chapters 2 and 3 provide basic information about the principles of library and resource organization, and subsequent chapters assume that readers are already familiar with this information. Through several examples, chapter 2 discusses limiting the topic, which for many students is the most difficult part of the literature search process. Chapter 3 concentrates on the principles of using online sources, including constructing a search strategy, using Boolean and phrase searching, and methods to expand and refine your results. Chapter 4 covers basic information about book literature, that is, catalogs to establish the presence of monographic material and finding these items in the library. Chapter 5 discusses PsycINFO and *Psychological Abstracts*, the most important indexes to the research literature of psychology.

Chapter 6 covers important indexes in the related areas of education, management, medicine, and sociology. Whereas chapters 5 and 6 concentrate on subject searches, chapter 7 discusses the author/citation search, which begins with a particular key source. No discussion of libraries is complete without mention of government publications, especially those of the U.S. federal government. These publications are described in chapter 8. Chapter 9 covers sources of information on psychological tests and measures. Chapter 10 presents some important but less frequently used basic sources of information: doctoral dissertations, book reviews, and biographical sources. Chapter 11 helps the individual who has exhausted the resources of his or her own library by providing alternative sources such as interlibrary loan and the Internet.

Library Use is intended to complement the content of other resources. Information on how to organize or write a paper is found in other works such as Booth, Colomb, and Williams (1995); Slade (1999); Sternberg and Leach (1993); and Turabian (1976). For discussion of the format of a psychology paper, proper reference style, and so forth, consult the 5th edition of the *Publication Manual of the American Psychological Association* (American Psychological Association, 2001). *Library Use* limits its scope to teaching about research that involves location of information in libraries and similar repositories. For discussion of approaches to empirical research—designing an experiment, constructing a questionnaire, collecting data, analyzing data, and so forth—you should consult books on research methods or statistics (e.g., Dyer, 1995; Kantowitz, Roediger, & Elmes, 2001; Kerlinger & Lee, 2000).

A NOTE ON LIBRARIES

The definition, location, and resources of the "typical" college library have changed dramatically over the past decade. A library used to be defined solely as a collection of materials located in one or more buildings containing printed books, journals, and reference materials. It also provided study space for users who used these sources on site. It still fulfills these functions, but a library does much more. With the development of electronic publishing, the definition of *library materials* has expanded to include books and journals that can be searched, read, downloaded, and printed in the library, home, office, or campus housing unit. Digital images of tables, graphs, charts, and illustrations can be obtained by users to create customized materials for use in reports and presentations. Use of computerized catalogs of holdings, electronic indexes, and other reference sources can substantially decrease the time required to locate articles and books. Although electronic access to research literature has decreased the amount of time needed to retrieve information, it has increased the need to review the search strategy to make it more efficient. It is also important to remember that older historical material may not be available in electronic formats.

Although the variety of publication formats owned by a library has changed, certain features of a library's content and organization have not. All libraries contain a monograph collection, consisting of books and series of books that you may borrow from the library. Every library uses some system to organize and identify monographs and to provide information about the items it owns in a catalog of its holdings, whether that catalog is electronic, in a traditional card catalog format, or both (see chapter 4).

Serials are publications issued on a regular or an irregular basis and may be in a printed or electronic format or both. The *Annual Review of Psychology,* published each year as a bound volume and as an electronic file, is a monographic serial. *American Psychologist,* a monthly journal, is another type of serial known as a periodical. *Psychological Abstracts* (see chapter 5), a reference tool indexing psychological literature, is published as a monthly periodical. Its machine-readable counterpart, PsycINFO, is updated weekly and is also a periodical. Printed volumes of periodicals may be classified and shelved with monographs, or they may be arranged alphabetically by periodical title. As with monographs, information about the serials your library receives, whether they are in printed or electronic format, is available in a catalog of holdings.

In addition, you may find that some research materials are available in your library solely in electronic formats. For example, many government publications are no longer widely distributed to libraries in paper. Instead, those publications are sent on electronic media (such as CD-ROM or DVD) or are available via the Internet. Libraries purchase electronic books and periodicals that they do not house on their shelves but to which they provide access electronically. Libraries can also purchase electronic "suites" of research tools that combine reference materials (like directories and encyclopedias), periodical indexes, and the complete text of selected journals. Like their paper counterparts, these materials are selected and made available because of their quality and usefulness to students and faculty. Electronic materials offer many advantages. Their cost and utility mean that even libraries serving small colleges can have access to a variety of research tools.

An increasing number of materials are available in electronic form. Some are merely electronic versions of publications that have been reviewed and edited, have scholarly value and, until recently, have appeared in a hard-copy form. Much of this book focuses on such materials. Chapter 11 addresses a new class of materials: electronic information on Web pages that has not previously appeared in print form. As discussed in chapter 11, these materials must be used with care, because anyone can publish a Web page, and the materials are not always reviewed or edited to ensure accuracy or validity.

All libraries contain staffs of librarians and library assistants and have similar functional departments, although these departments may have different names. The acquisitions or collection development department staff orders materials. The cataloging staff determines where materials should be located and how they are represented in the library's catalog of holdings. The staff of the serials department handles the mountain of daily, weekly, monthly, and annual journals and so forth. Reference librarians help users find what they need and provide instruction in library use. Interlibrary loan staff members locate and obtain copies of materials needed by researchers that are unavailable in the library. In sum, the goal of the library staff is to support the information needs of its community of users.

There are many ways to find out about your library. Most libraries distribute brochures or maintain Web sites that describe basic services, provide floor plans, list important contact information, and feature recent research materials acquired and services offered. Many libraries schedule brief tours or demonstrations at the beginning of each academic year. These not only help you to locate a library's main service areas (such as circulation and reserve) but also can introduce you to new services. Some libraries offer specialized workshops during the semester that cover literature in specific subject areas, the efficient use of electronic indexes, or hints on using the Internet effectively. Libraries are changing rapidly, and there is always something new to explore.

A NOTE ABOUT REFERENCE LIBRARIANS

In your search for information, you will probably have contact primarily with the reference staff. Conscientious reference librarians will be glad to assist you with your project; their job is to help people use library materials effectively, whether those materials are in traditional printed or new electronic format. Their specialty is information retrieval, not usually a subject such as psychology. As far as fields of study are concerned, librarians tend to be generalists rather than specialists. This general background provides them with a good overview of many fields, an understanding of how the fields relate to one another, and an ability to search for information in many ways and many places. They can assist you with using handbooks, bibliographies, dictionaries, encyclopedias, periodical indexes and abstracts, and catalogs of library holdings. If your search results in too much information, they can help you refine your search strategy. Conversely, they can offer advice on how to deal with a topic about which you are having trouble finding material or if items you locate at first are too technical. They can also be knowledgeable users of the Internet, including how search engines are compiled and the advantages and disadvantages of various search tools.

When you ask a librarian for assistance, be specific, complete, and timely about what you want. Requesting a particular index does not tell the librarian what you need, only what you think you need. Your list of search terms, the definition of your topic, and names of the relevant sources you have already identified may clarify your actual need.

Pressing librarians into service the day before a paper is due does not give them (or you) time to do a thorough job. Start early to allow yourself plenty of time and avoid the end-of-semester rush. By so doing, you enable a librarian to give your request more time and consideration.

Reference librarians often staff a centralized reference desk that offers in-person assistance. For questions that are difficult to field in a brief time at a reference desk, you may be able to schedule an appointment for a reference consultation. Librarians often answer brief questions by phone or electronic mail. Increasingly, libraries are using "chat" technology for interactive reference service. A library's Web site might be a helpful starting point at which to learn about these and other services. In addition, its Web site may supply subject-specific lists of reference tools, online tutorials, and other electronic resources that are useful if you need help when personal reference assistance is unavailable (such as late evening or early morning).

GETTING ORGANIZED: KEEPING TRACK OF YOUR SEARCH AND TAKING NOTES

An important part of the research process, and one too often overlooked, is keeping a record of your progress. Although this does take time, carefully documenting the sources of references, including accurate bibliographic information for each item reviewed, will save even more time in the long run. The need for this process becomes apparent as you complete your paper and organize reference lists and footnotes. As you review sources and gauge their relevance to your topic, you should also note the materials that you decide not to include in your paper. This can eliminate the possibility of hunting for references that you have already reviewed and dismissed as not relevant to your topic.

It is also important to identify the main points of the material you review and summarize them in your own words. You must read to understand the authors' points and not just copy the text. When you take notes, clearly identify exact quotations, taking care to indicate their source, including page numbers. Careful note-taking helps you to avoid inadvertent plagiarism. Put bluntly, plagiarism is theft. "Plagiarism is stealing other people's words and ideas and making them to appear to be your own" (Pauk, 1989, p. 379), and it may result in your failing a course or in your expulsion from college. Plagiarism is especially a problem when people "cut-and-paste" text from electronic sources to save time. Therefore, be sure to supply accurate and complete references to the sources of information and ideas contained in your paper. Gibaldi (1999) advised that if you have any doubt about whether something constitutes plagiarism, provide a reference.

As you examine materials, an essential task will be to record the bibliographic information of the sources you review. There are many ways to accomplish this. Sternberg and Leach (1993) recommended recording bibliographic information for each source examined on 3- by 5-in. cards and making notes on corresponding 5- by 7-in. "topic cards" about the content of sources. Another approach is to use bibliographic software such as EndNote, Library Master, or Noteworthy to document information about sources you review. Such software prompts you to include relevant information, can integrate bibliographic information with notes about each source, and often can format your reference list in standardized styles such as those used by the American Psychological Association or Modern Language Association. "Generic" database management software such as Microsoft Access or Filemaker Pro can also be used for this purpose. Recording bibliographic information and related notes in this manner is advantageous if you have ready access to a desktop or portable computer or a hand-held device. A disadvantage to this approach is that you may not have access to a computer when you examine a source.

When examining material, some people simply make photocopies of sources of interest, which can be useful if the exact wording is needed for a quotation. If many sources have been identified, however, photocopying can be very expensive, and the volume of information at your disposal may be overwhelming. In addition, as Slade (1999) points out, taking notes allows you to read the material carefully and organize the content in a way that suits your project rather than blindly following what is found in an article. If you take notes or make a photocopy of portions of a source, recording the complete citation with the notes or photocopy will save time in the long run as you use this information in writing your paper. Slade (1999) and Sternberg and Leach (1993) provide additional suggestions and details on taking notes, organizing content, and writing the paper.

Bibliographic information enables you to identify and locate a book, article, electronic document, or other information sources. For books, this information includes the names of the authors or editors, the title, the place of publication, the publisher, the date of publication, and the call number of the book and library from which the book was obtained. For journal articles, full bibliographic information includes the names of the authors, the article title, the journal name, the year, the volume number, the page numbers of the article, and the format if an electronic version is used. Sources of information that exist only in an electronic format require bibliographic information that is unique to the media; for example, Web pages require the uniform resource locator (URL) of the item, the date the material was created, and the date on which you accessed it, as well as other elements. Become accustomed to recording information as outlined in the *Publication Manual of the American Psychological Association*. Record the complete bibliographic information for each source. Such recording helps ensure accuracy and completeness and saves time later in the research process. In addition, record the source or reference tool in which you located the information about the article, book, or other publication. This information will be essential if you need to acquire an item on interlibrary loan (see chapter 11).

HOW TO USE THIS BOOK

At the beginning of the book, you will find a detailed table of contents, which contains a brief outline for each chapter. This table of contents indicates both the materials in and the organization of each chapter. At the beginning of each chapter, you will find the major sources discussed within that chapter listed in the order of their presentation. References to other materials in each discussion are listed at the end of the chapter. Within each chapter, tables and figures are identified by a double-numbering system that shows the chapter number and a sequential number for each table and figure. Some parts in the figures are identified with numbers. Rather than being presented in a key to each figure, these parts, or figure elements, are described and explained in the text, and the corresponding element reference number appears in boldface in the text.

Many of the research tools we discuss in this book are indexes to research literature published as journal articles and books. These indexes are usually in electronic formats and index the contents of hundreds—and sometimes thousands—of publications. The producers of these indexes frequently modify the years covered by the indexes by extending the coverage backward. For this reason, the date the computer index began often does not indicate the same initial dates of the publications it covers. Where these two dates differ, we elected to include the date of the earliest publications indexed when that date is known.

Throughout *Library Use*, we have emphasized that both knowledge of the bibliographic tools in psychology and search strategy are the keys to the successful literature search. The development of plans for systematic gathering of information is illustrated throughout the book within the context of the sources presented. For this reason, *Library Use* is more than a guide to the literature: It is a tool for learning.

REFERENCES

American Psychological Association. (2001). *Publication manual of the American Psychological Association* (5th ed.). Washington, DC: Author.

Booth, W. C., Columb, G. G., & Williams, J. M. (1995). *The craft of research*. Chicago: University of Chicago Press.

Dyer, C. (1995). *Beginning research in psychology: A practical guide to research methods and statistics*. Oxford, England: Blackwell.

Gibaldi, J. (1999). *MLA handbook for writers of research papers* (5th ed.). New York: Modern Language Association.

Kantowitz, B. H., Roediger, H. L., & Elmes, D. G. (2001). *Experimental psychology: Understanding psychological research*. Belmont, CA: Wadsworth.

Kerlinger, F. N., & Lee, H. B. (2000). *Foundations of behavioral research* (5th ed.). Fort Worth, TX: Harcourt.

Pauk, W. (1989). *How to study in college* (4th ed.). Boston: Houghton-Mifflin.

Slade, C. (1999). *Form and style: Research papers, reports, theses* (11th ed.). Boston: Houghton-Mifflin.

Sternberg, R. J., & Leach, C. (1993). *The psychologist's companion: A guide to scientific writing for students and researchers* (3rd ed.). Cambridge, England: Cambridge University Press.

Turabian, K. L. (1976). *A manual for writers of term papers, theses, and dissertations* (3rd ed.). Chicago: University of Chicago Press.

2 Selecting and Defining the Topic

Sources Discussed

Annual reviews
Handbooks
Textbooks

WRITING A paper should be a rewarding learning experience. It should involve you in gathering information, learning about a topic, evaluating ideas, examining issues, synthesizing information, and reaching conclusions. It should support your personal growth and assist in development of good work habits. The final product of your efforts should give you a sense of accomplishment.

Additionally, someone else—a professor, a thesis advisor, a conference program reviewer, or a journal reviewer—will read and evaluate your paper. Receiving positive and negative feedback on your work can help you become a more effective communicator. Achieving both personal and academic success in writing papers requires that you master each step of the process while avoiding several pitfalls.

IMPORTANCE OF SELECTING AND DEFINING A TOPIC

The first step in the research project is selecting, defining, and narrowing the topic. Success at this stage is essential for a high-quality paper. At times you may have little latitude because the topic has been assigned; at other times, you may have few constraints other than the length of the paper. In the latter case, you may find selecting a topic to be a difficult task. The topic you select should be interesting, manageable, and appropriate. Although we cannot tell you what topic to select, in this chapter we discuss some common mistakes that students make and present some suggestions for selecting, defining, and narrowing your topic.

GUIDELINES FOR SELECTING A TOPIC

Investigating and finally selecting a topic for a paper is a process that takes some time and careful consideration. As you begin this process, you should consider a topic that satisfies the following criteria:

- *It should be interesting.* The topic should be something about which you want to learn. Your interest may be piqued by a particular class lecture or a story in the media that is related to the class. It is important to remember that maintaining your motivation for a project is easier if you are enthusiastic about the topic.

- *It should be appropriate.* The topic should be directly relevant to your assignment. You should also have the background and knowledge to be able to read and understand the materials you find. A class project that is only tangentially related to the course will not be well received by an instructor. If in doubt about your topic, explore it with your instructor.

- *It should be manageable.* The topic must be sufficiently limited so that you can do a credible job in the time and space available. You will probably need to restrict your topic several times after selecting the initial topic area.

- *It should be researchable.* Conducting research on the topic should be feasible given the resources available to you. Again, consult those most familiar with the research resources on your campus (such as your instructor or a librarian) for advice.

Topic selection is covered in other research guides. For additional discussions, consult sources such as Booth, Colomb, and Williams (1995); Pauk (1989); Slade (1999); or Sternberg and Leach (1993).

PITFALLS TO AVOID

Numerous mistakes are possible in writing a paper. Some of the problems listed below have been noted by other authors (e.g., Booth, Colomb, & Williams, 1995; Kennedy, 1979; Pauk, 1989; Sternberg & Leach, 1993; Turabian, 1976); others are observations we have made. By being aware of these problems, you may be able to avoid them.

Topic Too Broad

A common mistake is writing a paper on a topic that is too broad. Although a textbook may cover topics such as stress, personality tests, or conflict in a few pages and refer to only a few citations, numerous books and articles have been written about each of these topics. You probably do not plan to write a book, so you will need to limit your topic. One way to limit your paper is to set a time and page restriction. Other ways of limiting the topic are presented later in this chapter. Unless the topic is well defined and restricted, you risk writing a paper that is superficial or poorly organized. Narrow your topic!

Abulia

Webster's Dictionary defines *abulia* as an "abnormal lack of ability to act or to make decisions" (Merriam-Webster's, 1999, p. 5). Students have several common sources of abulia:

1. Everything appears to be so interesting that selecting one topic seems impossible. If you find yourself in this situation, select several interesting topics, assign a number from 1 to 6 to each, and roll a die. If the decision of chance is not acceptable, then you really do have a preference. What is it?

2. Nothing looks interesting enough for a paper. If you feel this way, ask yourself why you enrolled in this course or why you need to write the paper. Did you find something interesting at the beginning? If the course is required, ask yourself what about the course is so important that it is considered essential. Then pick a topic that explores answers to these questions.

3. You may feel too poorly informed to select a good topic. Start skimming your textbook or the readings selected by your instructor. Read in detail sections that you find interesting and find other sources on the topic. Set a deadline for selecting your topic!

Procrastination

Library research takes time, and there are few shortcuts. Procrastination (putting it off until some future time) lessens your ability to be successful by limiting your time and potentially dictating concessions in quality. Alsip and Chezik (1974) reviewed four typical excuses students give for delaying: (a) "I don't have enough time now"; (b) "I'm in the wrong place," "It's too noisy or too quiet," and so on; (c) "Other things are more important"; and (d) "I'm not in the right mood." Some aspects of library research—especially getting started and selecting a topic—can be accomplished through a series of small actions and in a series of small time blocks. For example, finding a relevant book or copying a review article to get started takes only a few minutes in most college libraries. Divide your project into a number of small tasks, and prepare a task schedule. Stop wasting time!

Uninteresting Topic

If you have little interest in a topic, you may be tempted to throw the paper together at the last minute. Such a paper will probably be disorganized, superficial, poorly documented, poorly prepared, and unproofread. Such a paper will not only be a waste of time, it will probably receive a poor response from your readers. Start early, explore several alternative topics, and then select a topic that can sustain your interest through the ups and downs of research. Pick a topic that is interesting to you.

Inadequate Background

Some topics demand extensive knowledge of mathematics, biology, pharmacology, and so forth. For example, some students try to conduct their own surveys to support their paper topic. This sounds like a simple task but requires background in questionnaire design, sampling, and statistics, and the survey may be subject to review by a campus human subjects committee. Ask yourself the following questions about your topic: Do I have the background in this area to enable me to read and understand the literature on the topic? If not, will I gain the background as the course progresses, or will I have to learn this independently? Do I have the time to spend in such independent study? Is this kind of independent learning something that I am prepared to do now?

Topic Too Familiar

Sternberg and Leach (1993) comment,

> The purpose of student papers is for the student to learn something about some topic. It is therefore to the student's advantage to select a topic with which he [or she] is relatively (although not necessarily totally) unfamiliar. Students sometimes seek to optimize safety (or grades) rather than learning, however, choosing a topic with which they are quite familiar. (pp. 17–18)

Although selecting an unfamiliar area may result in a more difficult task, some professors react negatively to the practice of writing papers on the same topic for different courses and assume that the student who does so is lazy and is attempting to slide by with a minimum of effort. Other professors argue that students who do this are cheating themselves by not seeking a broad education. Thus, the personal and academic achievement of writing on a topic already extremely familiar is suspect. Select a topic about which you can learn something new.

Desire to Impress the Professor

Writing a paper is a way to integrate, evaluate, and organize your learning and communicate it to another person. Examine your motives for selecting the topic. Attempting to destroy a theory or to impress the professor with your brilliance may backfire. You may not have the time to read enough material to write an earth-shattering paper. Therefore, select a topic about which you yourself wish to learn.

Controversial Topic

The goal of most courses in psychology is cognitive or affective growth or both. When dealing with controversy, you may be tempted to find and to use uncritically sources that support your own point of view. Yet, as you become more involved with research, you will find that most topics are far more complex than you initially imagined. Such a discovery may lead you to examine your values and behaviors. The discovery of complexity, mixed with self-evaluation, may markedly increase the difficulty of your task. It may result in a positive experience if it leads to a paper of superior quality. It may, however, result in a negative experience if the complexity of the topic or your emotional involvement interferes with your completing the project. Turabian (1976) cautions that a controversial topic demands extreme care. The case must be stated clearly and precisely and must be supported heavily with documentation. Unless you have an open mind and a commitment to do thorough work, you would be well advised to avoid highly controversial topics.

Resources Unavailable

Very often the statement "There's nothing on my topic in the library" results from a student's inability to locate available material. There are, however, some areas in which very little has been written and very little research has been done. This may not be apparent until you begin preliminary reading and become involved in the literature search process. This reinforces our advice to begin the research process early and to consult your instructor for advice if you are unsure about where to begin.

Reliance on Secondary Sources

Some students find two or three books about a topic and proceed to write a paper based on these sources. This activity is not research; it is book reporting. In general, books (especially textbooks) are secondary sources, summarizing, interpreting, evaluating, and reporting the research and theorizing of others. Secondary sources are valuable as an introduction to a topic but should not be your sole source of information. Although books are usually accurate, an author may report inaccurately or may exclude an important piece of research because of misinterpretation, prejudice, misjudgment, or sloppy scholarship. Several articles (e.g., Brammel & Friend, 1981; Hogan & Schroeder, 1981; Samelson, 1974) have commented on the apparent inaccuracies in a number of authoritative, standard sources. Unless you read the original research as reported in the primary literature (such as journal articles or government reports), you cannot be certain that your reporting and evaluation are accurate.

Ignoring the Audience

Someone else will read your paper. What will make it interesting to read? Too often student papers are difficult to read and understand. Why? Some are poorly written: They are loaded with grammatical, spelling, punctuation, and other mistakes; one wonders if they were proofread. Others seem disorganized: It is difficult to tell where the author is heading; information does not seem to be organized into logical sections of information, and some parts are redundant. Other papers are just boring. As you prepare your paper, think about what you want to tell your readers and what you think they will find interesting.

DEFINING THE TOPIC

A clear, concise topic definition is essential for an effective literature search and a high-quality paper. Such a definition will provide guidelines for evaluating materials and determining their relevance or irrelevance to your topic. After spending hours of reading and taking notes, you may be tempted to include unessential information. Such inclusions may result in a disorganized, poorly focused paper. You can minimize this temptation by effectively defining your topic.

Slade (1999) suggests two ways of expressing a topic: (a) as a thesis statement or (b) as a question. For example, the following might be acceptable ways of initially defining a topic concerning occupational stress:

- *Thesis statement:* Occupational stress has a negative effect on interpersonal relations and thus adversely affects managers' job performance.
- *Question:* What is the effect of occupational stress on interpersonal relations in managers' job performance?

Either of these ways of expressing the topic might be acceptable; however, both are still fairly broad. What kinds of interpersonal relations—peer, supervisor, or subordinate relationships? What is meant by occupational stress? We need to take the next step and narrow a topic to a more manageable scope.

LIMITING THE TOPIC

You can narrow a topic in several ways. You may also make several iterations in refining the topic. Pauk (1989) suggests that every topic be subjected to three or four significant narrowings to reach a topic of manageable size. The following list, based in part on suggestions from Sternberg and Leach (1993), identifies a number of dimensions along which a topic may be limited.

Subject Population

You may restrict yourself to a particular population in several ways.

- *Age limitation:* You may be interested only in one particular age group, for example, infants, college students, or retirees.
- *Occupational group limitation:* You may be interested only in middle managers, secretaries, machinists, or school teachers.
- *Racial or ethnic limitation:* You may be interested only in Hispanic Americans, Asian Americans, or Irish Americans.
- *Species restriction:* In a learning, comparative, physiological, or ethological study, you might focus on rats, pigeons, chimpanzees, cats, dogs, chickens, or humans.

Theoretical Approach

You might limit a clinically oriented study to a behavior modification approach or to a Gestalt approach. For a study in human judgment, you might select from Bayesian, information integration, or policy-capturing approaches.

Research Methodology

You might limit consideration to a particular investigative method, for example, laboratory study, naturalistic observation, survey, or simulation. You might focus on use of a particular piece of equipment or a particular psychological test.

Content of Problem

In an information-processing topic, you might consider only studies of numerical, verbal, or pictorial information. In a study of perceptual illusions, you might limit yourself to a few particular illusions.

The method you use to limit your topic will depend heavily on the scope of your project and why you chose the paper subject. Topics might be constrained in very different ways for different reasons. For example, a project on personality may be restricted by type of methodology used for assessment, whereas a project on leadership may use different subject populations, such as senior managers versus first-line supervisors. The way you limit a topic depends on the judgments you make. But how and where can you begin?

SOURCES TO GET STARTED

After you have selected and defined a general topic, you are ready to begin the process of narrowing the topic. By consulting several types of general sources, you can get a general idea of the subject area, an overview of the topic, and several subtopics from which you might select. These general sources should also provide relevant references to begin your search for further information. This section discusses three types of general sources: (a) textbooks, (b) handbooks, and (c) annual reviews. To illustrate the use of these sources, we have selected three topics and will narrow each topic using one of the sources.

Textbooks

You might begin with your textbook. Read material relevant to your topic several times. This material may span an entire chapter with numerous references (a hint that the topic is broad and requires considerable limiting), or the material may be covered in a paragraph or two. Check sources that the author cites. Every good textbook will refer to important, relevant sources for all major topics covered, providing complete bibliographic information on each source. With those references, you can start a literature search and use those sources to find other materials. If, however, the topic that interests you is not addressed in your textbook, you may need to refer to another textbook. In gathering this information, you will find things that will help you limit your topic.

To illustrate limiting a topic, we consider a topic popular in social psychology, Festinger's Theory of Cognitive Dissonance. In their textbook *Social Psychology*, Aronson, Wilson, and Akert (1999) discuss this subject in chapter 6, "Self-Justification and the Need to Maintain Self-Esteem." They note that most people are reasonable, rational, moral individuals who wish to perceive themselves as behaving that way. When we perform an action that might seem inconsistent with that viewpoint (we might appear as irrational, unreasonable, or immoral), we may tend to feel uncomfortable.

This state of discomfort, known as cognitive dissonance, was proposed by Leon Festinger (1957). Festinger and others suggest that there are several ways in which we can reduce this state of dissonance. Within chapter 6 of *Social Psychology*, Aronson et al. (1999) provide several examples of dissonance-producing behaviors (e.g., smoking, decision making) and the need to justify our behaviors. They discuss several applications of the theory in viewing social problems (e.g., race relations, AIDS prevention). They also observe that we often hate our victims and comment that there is a large component of motivation: Arousal and discomfort drive individual behavior.

Much of the research on cognitive dissonance was conducted in the 1960s and 1970s. Beginning on page 217, the authors note that contemporary researchers have extended this body of work on individuals' need for self-justification (Gollweitzer & Wicklund, 1985; Higgins, 1987; Steele, 1988; Tesser, 1988).

If this were our topic, at this point we might limit our topic in several ways. We might select one of the newer theories, for example, focusing on self-evaluation maintenance theory (Tesser, 1988). We might further reduce the scope of our topic by focusing on

TABLE 2.1. Sequential Steps in Limiting a Topic in Social Psychology

Stage	Topic statement
Initial topic	Cognitive dissonance
1st narrowing	The need to maintain self-esteem
2nd narrowing	Self-evaluation maintenance theory
3rd narrowing	Helping strangers vs. friends in competitive situations where task outcome may affect self-esteem

the ways individuals behave in competitive situations when helping or not helping other people may affect our performance. This example of narrowing is shown in Table 2.1.

Handbooks

A second logical source for beginning a literature search and narrowing your topic is a handbook. Most good handbooks have several characteristics that make them well suited for this purpose.

- They provide an authoritative summary of a particular topic, including evaluations of theory and research.
- Experts in a field write them. The common practice is for one or more experienced scholars in a field to edit the contributions of several authors, each of whom writes about a special area of interest or expertise.
- They are usually written at a level for a beginning graduate student in a particular subfield and therefore assume that readers have some familiarity with a broad area of psychology.
- They are often more comprehensive than the typical textbook.
- They contain extensive reference lists.

There are also some disadvantages of using handbooks as a starting point.

- Handbooks are not available to cover all areas of psychology.
- Some areas are advancing so rapidly that handbooks can become obsolete very quickly.
- Some handbooks are better than others.

Suppose your topic is in the general area of child or developmental psychology. An outstanding source in this field that you might consult is the *Handbook of Child Psychology* (Damon, 1998). The fifth edition of this classic source is the product of numerous experts in the field of child psychology and lifespan developmental psychology. The four volumes contain more than 70 articles on theoretical models, cognition, perception, language, social development, emotional development, personality development, and practical applications in child psychology.

Suppose further that you are interested in development of problem-solving skills in children. Because this is within the domain of cognitive development, we turn to Volume 2, *Cognition, Perception, and Language*. Chapter 16, "Reasoning and Problem Solving," seems relevant (DeLoache, Miller, & Pierroutsakos, 1998). This 40-page chapter contains more than 200 references (nearly 8 pages) relevant to problem solving and child psychology.

DeLoache et al. (1998) suggested that, although Piagetian models of reasoning find children illogical when comparing their thought processes with a normative model, more recent research that approaches problems differently shows children to be more rational and capable of reasoning than previously believed. They argued that "what has been taken as evidence of structural deficits has turned out to stem instead from knowledge deficits" (p. 802).

DeLoache et al. (1998) focused their chapter on informal or everyday reasoning. They discuss different kinds of relations that serve as the basis for reasoning, problem solving, and scientific reasoning. Because we are interested in development of problem solving, we turn to the second section of the chapter. We find here that the authors have conceptualized several factors in problem solving—a goal, obstacles to achieving the goal, strategies that can be used, resources that may or may not be available, and evaluation of the outcomes of the problem-solving process.

The Piagetian approach to the concept of conservation of number focuses on the structure of the task. Has the child mastered the concept of number conservation, which we think should be acquired by about age 5, such that he or she understands that quantity is unrelated to arrangement and appearance of objects (Feldman, 2000, pp. 230–231)? Using the DeLoache et al. (1998) approach, however, we would consider conservation as a type of problem solving. We are referred to Siegler's (1995) research on training on nonconserving children. Siegler found that children used a variety of strategies. More important, DeLoache et al. (1998) suggested that deficiencies in problem solving may be caused by shortcomings in domain knowledge particular to the task at hand rather than to poor strategy. Other factors that may affect success in problem solving may include planning skills, social factors, and cultural factors. Pursuing this, we elect to investigate further the specific topic of changes of knowledge base as influences in problem-solving effectiveness in 5-year-old children (e.g., Chi, 1978; Schneider & Brun, 1987).

Thus, we have narrowed our topic. There appear to be several relevant references with which we can begin our search. We can see the successive limiting of topic scope in Table 2.2.

TABLE 2.2. Sequential Steps in Limiting a Topic in Child Psychology

Stage	Topic statement
Initial topic	Child cognitive development
1st narrowing	Problem solving in children
2nd narrowing	Informal or everyday reasoning in 5-year-old children
3rd narrowing	Impact of domain-specific knowledge on problem-solving effectiveness in 5-year-old children

At the end of this chapter, you will find a selected list of handbooks that might help you begin your literature search and narrow your topic.

Annual Reviews

A third important source of information is the annual review. Most important for psychologists is the *Annual Review of Psychology*. The first volume, containing 18 review articles, appeared in 1950. Since then, the annual volumes have included from 15 to 22 articles. As the field of psychology has expanded, reviews have become more focused, and new topics have been added. In the preface to volume 32, Rosenzweig and Porter (1981) summarized the intent of the series. They noted,

> Each volume is planned to present selective and evaluative reviews of status and recent progress in several main areas of psychology. . . . We try to follow . . . a Master Plan according to which some topics appear each year, some every other year, and some less frequently. (p. v)

A sampling of recent topics includes the following: social cognitive theory, adolescent development, personality, thinking, statistical graphs, olfaction, decision technology, thought suppression, negotiation, attitude change, and memory systems in the brain.

For illustrative purposes, suppose that our topic is the role of context in associative learning (classical conditioning). How did we get to that narrowed topic?

Most basic psychology textbooks distinguish between two primary approaches to learning: classical and operant conditioning (e.g., Lahey, 1998; Weiten, 2001). Classical conditioning traces its roots to work by Pavlov (1927). In the classical conditioning paradigm, learning occurs as an unconditioned stimulus (US; e.g., a puff of air) is paired with a conditioned stimulus (CS; e.g., a tone). With a sufficient number of pairings, organisms come to anticipate the US when the CS occurs, and behavior changes in response to the CS. In the previous example, human research subjects might come to make an unconditioned response such that they blink when the tone sounds. Classical conditioning has relevance to everyday experience in shaping the experience of emotions, such as fears.

In contrast, operant conditioning focuses on learning that occurs as a function of the consequences that are associated with responses. Operant conditioning, also known as instrumental learning, traces its roots to Edward Thorndike (1898) and was popularized by B. F. Skinner (1953). In the operant paradigm, we learn to behave based on the responses we receive to our behavior. Contingencies, or rules, determine whether and how behavior that is elicited will be reinforced or punished. As responses are reinforced, an association between response and reinforcement is acquired. Of course, conditioning is all much more complex than described here, but this is not intended as a book on learning.

Interested in classical conditioning, we turn to volume 52 of the *Annual Review of Psychology* and find a relevant review by Pearce and Bouton (2001) on associative learning. This review focuses on the impact of the theory of associative learning proposed by Rescorla and Wagner (1972). It reviews the Rescorla–Wagner (R–W) theory, subsequent research on the theory, and limits of the theory. The R–W theory is a quantitative theory that specifies the amount of change in association strength between the CS and US that will take place on any particular classical conditioning trial. It specifies that the amount of change in associative strength will be related to the difference between the current strength of all of the CSs present on a trial and the maximum degree of learn-

TABLE 2.3. Sequential Steps in Limiting a Topic in Learning

Stage	Topic statement
Initial topic	Learning
1st narrowing	Classical conditioning (associative learning)
2nd narrowing	Rescorla–Wagner (1972) theory of associative learning
3rd narrowing	Role of context in associative learning

ing possible with the US that is used. The R–W law specifies that changes in behavior should follow the classic negatively accelerated curve. R–W theory differs from earlier theories in that it allows for more than one stimulus in the role of CS. One important phenomenon that fits with R–W theory is blocking, whereby prior training with one element of a compound CS (e.g., CSA) may prevent the other element (e.g., CSB) from gaining associative strength.

Pearce and Bouton (2001) suggest that context in which conditioning, extinction, and recovery occur is important. For example, if conditioning occurs in one context and extinction in another, then returning to the original context results in some recovery from extinction. The work of Pearce and Bouton (2001) suggests that classical conditioning is a very complex phenomenon. Findings of research on context are not easy to explain; although contexts may not directly enter into a CS–US association, they appear to play a role in conditioning. Pearce and Bouton (2001) provide about 20 references to research on context. We have elected to narrow our focus to the role of context in associative learning.

Our steps in narrowing this topic are summarized in Table 2.3. Three notes are important. First, it may be useful to consult multiple annual review volumes for additional references or alternate interpretations. Second, some topics covered in annual review chapters are extremely complex and require extensive knowledge of the subdiscipline to comprehend them fully. Third, some topics in psychology demand extensive knowledge of other fields (e.g., brain physiology and biochemistry). As an illustration of this, many students would probably find Pearce and Bouton (2001) to be challenging reading.

Nothing should prevent you from using all three of these types of general sources to define and narrow your topic. Because textbooks, handbooks, and annual reviews cover topics selectively, discussing only a few of the many available resources, you can expect each to contain a different set of primary source materials. Furthermore, because each source is written by a different author, you can expect different points of view from each.

SELECTING SUBJECT-SEARCH TERMS

The next preliminary step in doing library research is developing a set of terms that will be used in conducting your literature search. When beginning research in a new area, students often search for information by subject. Most sources contain subject indexes. However, people, who have different perspectives and knowledge, compile indexes. The index for each source will be different and may use different terminology.

TABLE 2.4. Initial Lists of Search Terms for Sample Topics

Topic	Search terms	
Helping strangers vs. friends in competitive situations where task outcome may affect self-esteem	Self-esteem Competition Task outcome	Strangers Friends
Impact of domain-specific knowledge on problem-solving effectiveness in 5-year-old children	Children/childhood 5-year-olds/young children Strategy	Problem solving Domain knowledge Conservation
Role of context in associative learning	Associative learning Conditioning Context	Extinction Recovery Rescorla–Wagner theory

Determining in advance how a particular topic may be represented and indexed in the literature is not easy. For example, we might find the sample topic, problem solving in children, approached in several ways. In 1985, this would have been conceptualized by child psychologists within the context of Piaget's notions of conservation of number; thus, terms such as *conservation* would have been used to locate information. More recently, the problem of conservation in children is conceptualized by many child psychologists within the context of the development of problem-solving strategies.

You will need to compile a list of terms that you can use to locate relevant information on your topic. Include in this list any synonyms, technical terms, or important aspects of the topic of interest and how they relate to each other. The need for this will be more apparent as you begin your search of indexing tools. Compiling a list of key concepts and related terms is easier if you begin in the early stages of the process. As your search progresses, you may modify the list of terms to match the subject-indexing terms of the sources you are using.

Table 2.4 provides examples of the lists of search terms we might compile for the three sample topics illustrated in this chapter. Each list is different, just as each topic is very different.

SUMMARY STEPS IN DEFINING A TOPIC

The following is a brief review of the general steps in getting started. Although you might use a different sequence to suit your personal style, at some point each step will require attention.

- Select a general topic, being as specific as possible.
- Define the topic as a statement or question.
- Get an overview of the topic by reading a textbook, handbook, or annual review chapter.
- Limit the topic to a manageable size.
- Redefine and narrow the topic.
- Develop a list of possible search terms.

You are now ready to begin searching for additional information.

SELECTED HANDBOOKS

This list of handbooks is intended to be illustrative rather than exhaustive. The sources are grouped by general area. All of the handbooks identified here contain extensive lists of references. A few are a bit old; use them with care.

General Sources

Kazdin, A. E. (Ed.). (2000). *Encyclopedia of psychology* (Vols. 1–8). Washington, DC: American Psychological Association; and New York: Oxford University Press.

Keren, G., & Lewis, C. (Eds.). (1993). *A handbook for data analysis in the behavioral sciences* (Vols. 1–2). Hillsdale, NJ: Erlbaum.

Learning, Motivation, and Sensory Processes

Levinson, D., Ponzetti, J. J., & Jorgensen, P. F. (Eds.). (1999). *Encyclopedia of human emotions* (Vols. 1–2). New York: Macmillan.

Developmental, Personality, and Social

Bengtson, V. L., & Schaie, K. W. (Eds.). (1999). *Handbook of theories of aging.* New York: Springer.

Birren, J. E., & Schaie, K. W. (Eds.). (2001). *Handbook of the psychology of aging* (5th ed.). New York: Academic Press.

Damon, W. (Ed.-in-Chief). (1998). *Handbook of child psychology* (5th ed., Vols. 1–4). New York: Wiley.

Groth-Marnat, G. (Ed.). (1996). *Handbook of psychological assessment* (3rd ed.). New York: Wiley.

Sternberg, R. J. (Ed.). (1999). *Handbook of creativity.* New York: Cambridge University Press.

Sternberg, R. J. (Ed.). (2000). *Handbook of intelligence.* New York: Cambridge University Press.

Clinical, Counseling, Educational, and Industrial/Organizational

Berliner, D. C., & Calfee, R. C. (1996). *Handbook of educational psychology.* New York: Macmillan.

Carson-DeWitt, R. (Ed.). (2001). *Encyclopedia of drugs, alcohol, and addictive behavior* (rev. ed., Vols. 1–4). New York: Macmillan.

Cassell, D. K., & Gleaves, D. H. (2000). *The encyclopedia of obesity and eating disorders* (2nd ed.). New York: Facts on File.

Dell Orto, A. E., & Marinelli, R. P. (Eds.). (1995). *Encyclopedia of disability and rehabilitation.* New York: Macmillan.

REFERENCES

Alsip, J. E., & Chezik, D. D. (1974). *Research guide in psychology*. Morristown, NJ: General Learning Press.

Aronson, E., Wilson, T. D., & Akert, R. M. (1999). *Social psychology* (3rd ed.). New York: Longman.

Booth, W. C., Colomb, G. G., & Williams, J. M. (1995). *The craft of research*. Chicago: University of Chicago Press.

Bramel, D., & Friend, S. V. (1981). Hawthorne, the myth of the docile worker, and class bias in psychology. *American Psychologist, 36,* 867–878.

Chi, M. T. H. (1978). Knowledge structures and memory development. In R. S. Siegler (Ed.), *Children's thinking: What develops?* (pp. 73–96). Hillsdale, NJ: Erlbaum.

Damon, W. (1998). *Handbook of child psychology* (5th ed., Vols. 1–4). New York: Wiley.

DeLoache, J. S., Miller, K. F., & Pierroutsakos, S. L. (1998). Reasoning and problem solving. In W. Damon (Series Ed.), & D. Kuhn & R. S. Siegler (Vol. Eds.), *Handbook of child psychology: Vol. 2. Cognition, perception, and language* (5th ed., pp. 801–850). New York: Wiley.

Feldman, R. S. (2000). *Development across the life span* (2nd ed.). Upper Saddle River, NJ: Prentice-Hall.

Festinger, L. (1957). *A theory of cognitive dissonance*. Evanston, IL: Row, Peterson.

Gollwitzer, P. M., & Wicklund, R. A. (1985). Self symbolizing and the neglect of others' perspectives. *Journal of Personality and Social Psychology, 48,* 702–715.

Higgins, E. T. (1987). Self-discrepancy: A theory relating self and affect. *Psychological Review, 94,* 319–340.

Hogan, R., & Schroeder, D. (1981, July). Critique: Seven biases in psychology. *Psychology Today,* 8–14.

Kennedy, J. R. (1979). *Library research guide to education: Illustrated search strategies and sources*. Ann Arbor, MI: Pierian Press.

Lahey, B. M. (1998). *Psychology: An introduction* (6th ed.). Boston: McGraw-Hill.

Merriam-Webster's collegiate dictionary (10th ed.). (1999). Springfield, MA: Merriam-Webster.

Pauk, W. (1989). *How to study in college* (4th ed.). Boston: Houghton-Mifflin.

Pavlov, I. P. (1927). *Conditioned reflexes*. London: Oxford University Press.

Pearce, J. M., & Bouton, M. E. (2001). Theories of associative learning in animals. *Annual Review of Psychology, 52,* 111–139.

Rescorla, R. A., & Wagner, A. R. (1972). A theory of Pavlovian conditioning: Variations in the effectiveness of reinforcement and non-reinforcement. In A. H. Vlack & W. F. Prokasy (Eds.), *Classical conditioning II: Current research and theory* (pp. 64–99). New York: Appleton-Century-Crofts.

Rosenzweig, M. R., & Porter, L. W. (Eds.). (1981). *Annual Review of Psychology, Vol. 32*. Palo Alto, CA: Annual Reviews.

Samelson, F. (1974). History, origin myth, and ideology: "Discovery" of social psychology. *Journal of the Theory of Social Behavior, 4,* 217–231.

Schneider, W., & Brun, H. (1987). The role of context in young children's memory performance: Istomina revisited. *British Journal of Developmental Psychology, 5,* 333–341.

Siegler, R. S. (1995). How does change occur: A microgenetic study of number conservation. *Cognitive Psychology, 28*, 225–273.

Skinner, B. F. (1953). *Science and human behavior.* New York: Macmillan.

Slade, C. (1999). *Form and style: Research papers, reports, theses* (11th ed.). Boston: Houghton-Mifflin.

Steele, C. M. (1988). The psychology of self-affirmation: Sustaining the integrity of the self. In L. Berkowitz (Ed.), *Advances in experimental social psychology* (Vol. 21, pp. 261–302). New York: Academic Press.

Sternberg, R. J., & Leach, C. (1993). *The psychologist's companion: A guide to scientific writing for students and researchers* (3rd ed.). Cambridge, England: Cambridge University Press.

Tesser, A. (1988). Toward a self-evaluation maintenance model of social behavior. In L. Berkowitz (Ed.), *Advances in experimental social psychology,* (Vol. 21, pp. 181–227). New York: Academic Press.

Thorndike, E. L. (1898). Animal intelligence: An experimental study of the associative processes in animals. *Psychological Monographs, 24*(8), 1–109.

Turabian, K. L. (1976). *A manual for writers of term papers, theses, and dissertations* (3rd ed.). Chicago: University of Chicago Press.

Weiten, W. (2001). *Psychology: Themes and variations* (5th ed.). Belmont, CA: Wadsworth.

3 Computer Searching

RATIONALE FOR A COMPUTER SEARCH

IN THE chapters that follow, we discuss many types of sources and tools for locating research, review, biographical, and other types of information. Such information appears in the form of books, journals, and electronic media. It is accessed with bibliographic tools, many of which are specific to particular academic disciplines. This chapter focuses on the general methodology for conducting a computer search regardless of the discipline, tool, or form of information. Throughout this book, we focus heavily on computer searches because of their increasing availability, their ability to conduct a more focused search, and their ability to perform a search quickly.

As early as the 1960s, many publishers relied on computerized methods to produce printed reference tools, including periodical indexes. At about the same time, libraries began to utilize computers to produce card catalogs or records of their collections of books and other materials. Most researchers were limited to using printed periodical indexes and library card files to locate books, journal articles, book reviews, tests, dissertations, and other information. Using these indexes and catalogs was time-consuming and inefficient, and sometimes the results were incomplete. It was especially difficult if a topic combined several concepts, was interdisciplinary in nature, or was represented by terms that were not yet part of a discipline's jargon. Using these printed indexes and catalogs to the research literature was largely limited to access by author names, titles, and subjects.

Shortcomings of print indexes and their thesauri are numerous. Successful subject access depended on a reliable, well-constructed index and its controlled vocabulary. The controlled vocabulary is documented in a thesaurus of subject–search terms, from which subject terms are selected to represent each article in an index or book in a library catalog. Only terms in a thesaurus (e.g., *Thesaurus of Psychological Index Terms*, *Library of Congress Subject Headings*) could be attached to each article or book to describe its subject content. Controlled vocabularies were slow to incorporate new subject headings with new terminology from emerging research areas. Subject terms are assigned by human indexers. The decision as to which terms and how many terms are assigned depend on the skills, judgment, and experience of those indexers. Furthermore, the subject content of each article or book is represented by only a few subject terms.

In the 1990s, advances in information storage, computer processing speeds, desktop computing, and distributed systems brought these electronic databases out of the back rooms of publishers and libraries and delivered them to the computers of individual researchers. Flexible software interfaces make citations to research literature easy to search, display, and download or print. This enables relatively quick access to information, and search results can be easily modified to the needs of the individual researcher. Many of the principles needed to conduct computer searches of periodical indexes and library catalogs can be applied to searching the increasing number of full-text electronic journals.

What does a computer search do? Starting with an electronic database of information, a search uses a piece of computer software to look for particular information in that electronic database. In a search specification, the user defines what he or she is searching: what fields in the database to check and what information to seek. Then the search interrogates the database to see if the content in the database matches the particular information contained in the search specification. The search attempts to match the specific terms provided in the query with terms contained in the various fields of records in the database. Each time the search identifies a record in the database that matches the parameters in the search specification, the document will be added to the list of hits. The results of a search reported to the user will include any information contained in the database that matches the search specification provided by the user (document "hits").

Unfortunately, relying solely on electronic indexes is not always possible. For example, some computerized indexes and library catalogs only contain citations to recent material, and a complete retrospective literature search requires the use of printed indexes. This may be important when researching the history of an area or the development of concepts. In addition, constructing a logical, well-considered search strategy is essential to a successful computer search. It is also important to invest time in defining your topic, as discussed in chapter 2.

BIBLIOGRAPHIC RECORD

Any document can be described using several types of standard attributes, regardless of the document's form, length, or type. This information is compiled in what is known as a bibliographic record. This record is a surrogate, describing the document and differentiating it from all other documents. There are many types of information that may appear in a document's bibliographic record. Depending on the nature of the document, the bibliographic record could specify the size of the physical document; the institutional affiliation of the author; the language in which the document is published; the type of population used in the study; the age group of subjects in the study; or a unique accession number, which is assigned to each document in the database. Some of the most common elements found in the bibliographic record of any type of database for any type of document include the following:

Author. This is the person or persons who wrote the document.

Title. This is the name of the document.

Source. This is the title of a document that contains a number of shorter pieces. It may be a journal, serial, or handbook. This is sometimes the journal name and includes the volume, issue, and page numbers of the document.

Year. This is the year the document was published.

Publisher. Especially with books, it may be important to know the name and location (city, state) of the institution that published the document.

Abstract. This is a brief summary of the contents of the document. It may be the summary provided by the author that appears at the beginning of a journal article.

Subject/keyword. These are terms from the thesaurus used by the index to identify key concepts in the document.

Accession number. This is a unique identifying code that differentiates one bibliographic record from all others in the database.

As previously noted, one of the problems with hard-copy printed databases is that they tend to limit ways in which information can be accessed. Most print indexes provide access based on only three criteria: author, title, and subject/keyword. With computer databases, it is often possible to construct a search that includes other fields of information, such as the abstract or the year of publication. By searching the abstracts within a database, for example, one is neither restricted to the terms from a controlled vocabulary nor confined by how those terms are assigned to documents by indexers. Therefore, a computer can improve the quality of a search by retrieving documents that might have been missed in a search of a printed or electronic subject index.

Before we begin discussing the mechanics of a computer search, we identify a topic in order to provide context.

CHAPTER EXAMPLE: EATING DISORDERS

Eating disorders are complex conditions that may include psychological, physical, and social components. There are three primary types of eating disorders: anorexia nervosa, bulimia nervosa, and binge eating. It is estimated that approximately 3% of young women develop anorexia or bulimia (Becker, Grinspoon, Klibanski, & Herzog, 1999). The majority of cases of eating disorders (90%) are women (Hoffman & Sargent, 1993). However, Philpott and Sheppard (1998) argued that eating disorders in men appear to be underreported. Eating disorders can be life threatening (Herzog et al., 1999). The mortality rate from anorexia is estimated by Sullivan (1995) at 5.9%, 0.56% per year, or 5.6% per decade, based on a meta-analysis of 42 published studies.

Common to both anorexia and bulimia is an obsession with being thin (Carney & Andersen, 1996). Individuals have a distorted sense of body image. They typically have been involved in dieting and weight loss programs. Unfortunately, not all people with eating disorders recognize or admit they have a problem (Hoffman & Sargent, 1993).

Anorexia nervosa is characterized by low body weight (less than 85% of expected weight), an intense fear of weight gain, an inaccurate perception of body weight, an obsession with food, and a severe restriction of food intake to the point of starvation (Hoffman & Sargent, 1993). Additional symptoms and complications include amenorrhea (lack of menstrual function) in women, hypotension (low blood pressure), bradycardia (low heart rate), anemia, intolerance to cold, and excessive thirst (Beaumont, 1988; Carney & Andersen, 1996; Hoffman & Sargent, 1993; Hsu, 1990).

Bulimia nervosa is marked by recurrent episodes of binge eating followed by inappropriate compensatory activities to eliminate food through self-induced vomiting, laxative abuse, enemas, or obsessive excessive exercise. The binge eating and compensation occur on average twice a week (Thelen, Mintz, & Vander Wal, 1996). Like people with anorexia, individuals with bulimia have a high standard of body thinness and an obsession with food. Some individuals with bulimia may be able to hide their condition for a long time because frequent binging helps them keep their body weight within the normal range (Hoffman & Sargent, 1993). Additional complications of bulimia may include dental erosion, inflammation of the esophagus, irregular menstrual periods, cramps, and rebound constipation (Hoffman & Sargent, 1993). People with bulimia may experience clinical depression, anxiety, obsessive–compulsive disorder, and other psychological problems (Herzog et al., 1999; Hoffman & Sargent, 1993).

Binge eating, the third major type of eating disorder, has also been newly recognized. It is characterized by episodic uncontrolled consumption of food, but it is not accompanied by compensatory activities such as self-induced vomiting to prevent weight gain. Binge eaters report feeling out of control during their eating episodes, characterized by unusually rapid eating, eating when not hungry, and eating past the point of physical discomfort (Devlin, 1996).

Athletes, especially women participating in organized sports in which there is pressure to achieve some prescribed body weight, may be susceptible to eating disorders, particularly anorexia nervosa and bulimia nervosa (Beals, Brey, & Gonyou, 1999). Eating disorders among athletes are a special concern for coaches and trainers as well as for sport psychologists, who need to be aware of the potential for this situation when working with athletes and teams (Sherman & Thompson, 2001).

Treatment of eating disorders appears most successful with early diagnosis. Denial of eating disorders, however, is often a problem (Hoffman & Sargent, 1993). Tools for assessment and diagnosis of eating disorders include the Interview for Diagnosis of Eating Disorders (Kutlesic, Williamson, Gleaves, Barbin, & Murphy-Eberenz, 1998) and the Expert System–Based Computer-Assisted Training program (Todd, 1996). Treatment may involve cognitive–behavior therapy (Kleifield, Wagner, & Halmi, 1996), pharmacotherapy (Jimerson, Wolfe, Brotman, & Metzger, 1996), nutritional counseling (Rock & Curran-Celentano, 1996), psychosocial interventions or, in the event of a severe case, hospitalization (American Psychiatric Association Work Group on Eating Disorders, 2000).

As we discuss how to define a search, we focus on the example of eating disorders. There are many aspects of the problem on which we might focus if we were to narrow our topic. We might want to identify more information on a particular type of eating disorder, for example, anorexia nervosa. We might wish to examine a particular aspect of the problem, such as diagnosis or treatment, or even a particular type of treatment. We might choose to focus on athletes, or we might wish to differentiate on the basis of gender.

CONSTRUCTING A SEARCH STRATEGY

Using our eating disorders example, assuming that we have defined and narrowed our topic as discussed in chapter 2, let us construct a search strategy. We start by identifying the general conceptual domains spanned by our topic. There are five general concepts in which we are interested: eating disorders, diagnostic approach, treatment methods, athletes, and gender. Three general types of eating disorders have been defined: anorexia nervosa, bulimia nervosa, and binge eating. For each of these concepts it is important to identify synonymous and related terms. By doing this, we can expand our search to cover the different ways in which authors or indexers might have addressed our

TABLE 3.1. Concepts and Potential Search Terms Related to Eating Disorders

General concept	Subconcept	Search terms, including related terms and synonyms
Eating disorders	Anorexia nervosa, bulimia nervosa, binge eating	Eating disorders, appetite disorders, anorexia, anorexia nervosa, bulimia, bulimia nervosa, binge eating
Diagnostic approach		Diagnosis, testing, assessment
Treatment methods		Treatment, cognitive behavior therapy, nutrition counseling, nutrition therapy, pharmacotherapy, psychosocial
Athletes		Athletes, athletics, sports
Gender		Men, women, male, female

topic. For example, some authors may have focused on sports (the activity), whereas others may have focused on athletes (the people involved), although either might be relevant. Table 3.1 identifies these concepts together with related terms we might need to use in our search. Let us start by assuming that we have a database containing a set of documents.

Using Boolean operators such as **AND**, **OR**, and **NOT**, we can combine our search terms in a number of ways to select various subsets of documents from the database. Using the **AND** operator to link two terms (two sets) will yield an intersecting subset of documents. In an intersection, both terms must be assigned to a document, and any document that does not include both terms would be excluded, as shown in the Venn diagram in Example 1 of Figure 3.1. Using the **OR** operator to link two terms (two sets) will yield a set that is a union of all documents that include either or both of the terms as shown in the Venn diagram in Example 2. Using the **NOT** operator to link two terms (two sets) will yield a subset that includes all documents containing term X but excluding any document that contains term Y as shown in the Venn diagram in Example 3. In a computer search, we can conveniently extend this logic to multiple terms and multiple Boolean operators within the same search.

To make this a bit more concrete, suppose we have a hypothetical online library of 1 million documents. Let us also suppose that the subjects of those documents occurred with the frequencies noted in Table 3.2. If we conducted a computer search of our database on only one of these terms, we would identify a large number of documents, many of which might not be of interest. For example, if we searched using the term *athletes,* we would identify 4,500 documents in our database, whereas if we searched using the term *women,* we would identify more than 10,000 documents. By searching in this fashion, we would have to review 5,800 documents on eating disorders, 6,300 documents on anorexia, 5,000 documents on bulimia, and an additional 1,200 documents on binge eating. Some of these might overlap, but in the printed (paper) version of our database, we would have to review each of the entries. This would be like constructing a Boolean search using the **OR** operator to combine terms into a union of all documents containing any of these terms—*eating disorders* **OR** *anorexia* **OR** *bulimia* **OR** *binge eating.* This

Example #1. Use of "**AND**."

Example #2. Use of "**OR**."

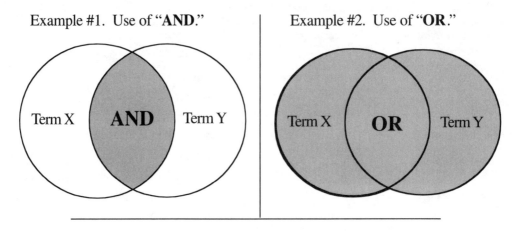

Example #3. Use of "**NOT**."

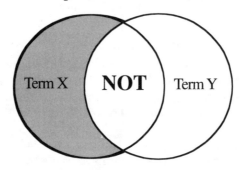

FIGURE 3.1. Boolean combination examples.

search would yield 5,800 + 6,300 + 5,000 + 1,200 document entries in our database, for a total of 18,300 documents to be reviewed—a pretty daunting task.

Suppose instead that we constructed our search combining several terms using a Boolean structure with **AND** operators. Let us restrict our search to documents that contain the terms *eating disorders* **AND** *athletes* **AND** *women*. We might find search results more like the outcomes shown in Table 3.3 (p. 34). By combining these three terms, our search yields a subset consisting of 30 documents. This is a reasonable number of documents to review.

If we became still more focused on the effectiveness of cognitive–behavior therapy in women athletes diagnosed with anorexia, our hypothetical search might consist of the combination of the terms *anorexia* **AND** *cognitive–behavior therapy* **AND** *athletes* **AND** *women*. However, if we wanted to compare effectiveness of cognitive–behavior therapy with nutrition therapy in women athletes diagnosed with anorexia, we would have to add **AND** *nutrition therapy* to our search strategy, reducing the number of documents retrieved in our search still further. Each time we add a term with **AND** to our search to make it more specific, we reduce the number of documents retrieved.

On the other hand, we are often concerned about use of alternate terms, in which case we might modify our search using the **OR** operator. For example, some authors may have used the term *athletes*, and others may have referred to participants in *sports*. Such a search would refer to *athletes* **OR** *sports*. Certain authors might have writ-

TABLE 3.2. Hypothetical Database of Documents Showing Distribution of Concepts Associated With Documents in the Database

Concept	Frequency
Eating disorders	5,800
Anorexia nervosa	6,300
Bulimia nervosa	5,000
Binge eating	1,200
Diagnostic approach	>10,000
Diagnosis	>10,000
Treatment methods	>10,000
Cognitive–behavior therapy	1,000
Nutrition	3,700
Nutrition counseling	22
Pharmacotherapy	3,300
Psychosocial therapy	21
Athletes	4,500
Sports	5,100
Gender	>10,000
Men	>10,000
Women	>10,000

ten about *women*, whereas others might have reported on *females*—again, an opportunity to use the **OR** operator. In general, using the **OR** operator expands our search.

A third type of pattern is the exclusion of a certain set of cases. Suppose we wish to focus on binge eaters. However, we are aware that individuals with bulimia engage in binge eating but then take countermeasures. In this case we are not interested in studies on people with bulimia and want to exclude them from our review. We might construct a search using the **NOT** operator: for example, *binge eating,* **NOT** *bulimia.* This would yield a set of documents that address binge eating but not the problem of bulimia.

Returning to our earlier search, comparison of the effectiveness of cognitive–behavior therapy as compared with nutrition therapy in women athletes diagnosed with anorexia, suppose we wish to make it as restrictive and yet as complete as possible. We want to use both alternate terms to expand our search with **OR** operators and yet restrict our search to certain concept domains using **AND** operators. Conceptually, it might look like the search represented by the Venn diagram in Figure 3.2 (p. 35). As we construct our database search on the computer, it might look like the following:

> (*anorexia* **OR** *anorexia nervosa*) **AND** *cognitive–behavior therapy* **AND** *nutrition*
> *therapy* **AND** (*athletes* **OR** *sports*) **AND** (*women* **OR** *woman* **OR** *female* **OR** *females*)

Note the use of parentheses in the preceding example to combine related terms using the **OR** operator. Much as in a mathematical expression where there is an implied order of operations (multiplication and division before addition and subtraction) as well as

TABLE 3.3. Search of a Hypothetical Database of Documents Combining Search Terms With Boolean Operators

Concept	Frequency
Eating disorders	5,800
Athletes	4,500
Women	>10,000
Eating disorders **AND** athletes	130
Eating disorders **AND** women	1,400
Athletes **AND** women	300
Eating disorders **AND** athletes **AND** women	30

moving left to right through the equation, if one wishes to deviate from the rule, the deviation must be specified. This search yields a subset of documents in which each one mentions each major concept in our search strategy.

CAVEATS AND NOTES

Wild Cards

Some search software will allow you to use a wild-card extension on a term for multiple alternatives. For example, some use the asterisk (*) as a wild card: for example, *sport** will find all of the following: *sport, sports,* and *sporting.* In other databases, use of the question mark (?) or a dollar sign ($) as a wild card is allowed. Some database search software does not use wild cards. For each database you use, find out whether the search software enables wild cards, what symbols are permitted, and how to use them. Most databases have an online set of instructions or hints about use. You will be informed which Boolean operators are used in the system, which wild cards are used, and which hints can help you structure your search.

Adjacent Terms

Some search software allows you to specify that terms must appear adjacent to each other. This is accomplished by using the **ADJ** operator. For example, *eating* **ADJ** *disorders* would require that both terms be in a bibliographic record and that the terms be used together in this order. Some search systems recommend reinforcing the adjacency of two words by using parentheses, for example (*eating* **ADJ** *disorders*). Thus, an article on "the prevalence of *eating disorders* in college women" would be included in your search, whereas an article on "*eating* preferences and reflux *disorders* in college women" would be excluded.

Number of References

Computers are amazing. In a very brief time they can identify many documents in a database that might be relevant to the search you specified. However, if you do a

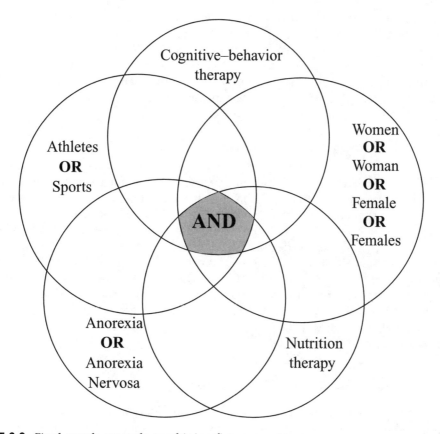

FIGURE 3.2. Final search example combining five concepts.

poor job of articulating exactly what information you desire, your search can return hundreds or thousands of documents that are irrelevant to your true needs. This will defeat your goal of saving time, because you now need to review many documents to find the few relevant ones. It is better to define your topic carefully, identify the key concepts as outlined in this chapter and in chapter 2, and think through your search strategy before you start keying your search into the computer.

Literalness

Computers conduct a search exactly as you have specified it. Some database search software differentiates between *women* and *woman,* but it is best to specify both terms if this is what you want, or use a wild card in *wom*n* if this is allowed. Typographical errors, such as *bulemia* instead of the correct term *bulimia,* will result in missing many important documents.

Fields to Search

As noted, you may elect to search for a work by a particular author or search for a title or a particular subject. Searching for an author may be useful if a person has conducted a large number of studies in an area and is a recognized expert in the field or contributed an important theoretical concept. Searching by title relies on your knowledge of a particular work that is important. To take advantage of either of these approaches, you must already have some knowledge of the field you wish to investigate. The power of a computer search is in the ability to search other fields in the database, such as the abstract, and to search using terms not contained in the controlled vocabulary of the database index.

Interfaces

Each database you use is presented through a computer software user interface that will structure your search and enable you to negotiate the search process and to review documents retrieved by your search. There are, however, many search software packages. Not only do they work differently, but their appearance also differs on the computer screen. You must be flexible as you move from database to database and search engine to search engine. In the remainder of this book, we present simplified examples of the user interface screens you will see. Expect, however, that what you see on the computer screen may not be exactly what you see in the figures in the pages of this book. The difference may occur because the database has been changed by the database publisher since this book was written, because the vendor of the service you are using has modified the user interface, or for any number of other reasons.

Online Help Systems and Tutorials

An increasing number of databases provide users with interesting and helpful assistance. Many provide a tutorial in which components of the system are illustrated and explained. Some also provide illustrations of search strategies and rules to be used in searching.

In later chapters, we describe various sources of bibliographic information, focusing heavily on computer searches of these sources and using the information given in this chapter to structure our search examples.

REFERENCES

American Psychiatric Association Work Group on Eating Disorders. (2000, January). *Practice guideline for the treatment of patients with eating disorders* (2nd ed.). Retrieved March 4, 2002, from http://www.psych.org/clin_res/guide.bk42301.cfm.

Beals, K. A., Brey, R. A., & Gonyou, J. B. (1999). Understanding the female athlete triad: Eating disorders, amenorrhea, and osteoporosis. *Journal of School Health, 69,* 337–340.

Beals, K. A., Brey, R. A., & Gonyou, J. B. (1999, October). Understanding the female athlete triad: Eating disorders, amenorrhea, and osteoporosis. *Journal of School Health, 69,* 337–340.

Beaumont, P. J. V. (1988). Recent advances concerning eating disorders. *Current Opinion in Psychiatry, 1,* 155–164.

Becker, A. E., Grinspoon, S. K., Klibanski, A., & Herzog, D. B. (1999). Eating disorders. *New England Journal of Medicine, 340,* 1092–1098.

Carney, C. P., & Andersen, A. E. (1996). Eating disorders: Guide to medical evaluation and complications. *Psychiatric Clinics of North America, 19,* 657–679.

Devlin, M. J. (1996). Assessment and treatment of binge-eating disorder. *Psychiatric Clinics of North America, 194,* 761–772.

Herzog, D. B., Dorer, D. J., Keel, P. K., Selwyn, S. E., Ekeblad, E. R., Flores, A. T., et al. (1999). Recovery and relapse in anorexia and bulimia nervosa: A 7.5-year follow-up study. *Journal of the American Academy of Child and Adolescent Psychiatry, 38,* 829–837.

Hoffman, L., & Sargent, M. (1993). *Eating disorders* (NIH Publication 94-3477). Washington, DC: National Institute of Mental Health.

Hsu, L. K. G. (1990). *Eating disorders.* New York: Guilford Press.

Jimerson, D. C., Wolfe, B. E., Brotman, A. W., & Metzger, E. D. (1996). Medications in the treatment of eating disorders. *Psychiatric Clinics of North America, 19,* 739–754.

Kleifield, E. I., Wagner, S., & Halmi, K. A. (1966). Cognitive–behavioral treatment of anorexia nervosa. *Psychiatric Clinics of North America, 19,* 715–737.

Kutlesic, V., Williamson, D. A., Gleaves, D. H., Barbin, J. M., & Murphy-Eberenz, K. P. (1998). The interview for the diagnosis of eating disorders—IV: Application to DMS–IV diagnostic criteria. *Psychological Assessment, 10,* 41–48.

Philpott, D., & Sheppard, G. (1998). More than mere vanity: Men with eating disorders. *Guidance and Counseling, 13*(4), 28–33.

Rock, C. L., & Curran-Celentano, J. (1996). Nutritional management of eating disorders. *Psychiatric Clinics of North America, 19,* 701–713.

Sherman, R. T., & Thompson, R. A. (2001). Athletes and disordered eating—Four major issues for the professional psychologist. *Professional Psychology: Research and Practice, 32,* 27–33.

Sullivan, P. F. (1995). Mortality in anorexia nervosa. *American Journal of Psychiatry, 152,* 1073–1074.

Thelen, M. H., Mintz, L. B., & Vander Wal, J. S. (1996). The bulimia test—revised: Validation with DSM–IV criteria for bulimia nervosa. *Psychological Assessment, 8,* 219–221.

Todd, L. K. (1996). A computer-assisted expert system for clinical diagnosis of eating disorders: A potential learning tool for practitioners. *Professional Psychology: Research and Practice, 27,* 184–187.

4 Locating a Book

Sources Discussed

Library Catalog

THIS CHAPTER discusses procedures for identifying and locating books (librarians refer to them as *monographs*) in the library. Monographs appear in many formats: single-volume books (e.g., *Library Use*), multiple-volume sets (e.g., *Handbook of Perception*), annual series (e.g., *Annual Review of Psychology*), and so forth. Some books contain important new contributions to the theoretical literature of a subject area, others contain original empirical contributions, still others contain a series of chapters prepared by experts in the field, and some contain extensive bibliographies or reviews of the literature. Books, however, are limited in several ways: They may present the point of view of only one author. Because writing and publishing a book is a time-consuming process, the book may not contain the most recent research. Therefore, books should be only a part of your literature search. You will need to supplement books with other materials, such as journal articles, as discussed in later chapters.

CHAPTER EXAMPLE: EMOTIONAL INTELLIGENCE

The subject of intelligence has been of interest to psychology students, practitioners, and scholars for more than a century. Until recently, most work on intelligence concentrated on cognitive capacities. Early work focused on attempts to measure cognitive intelligence. This view of intelligence tended to focus on verbal and numerical–logical abilities, and their measures tended to correlate with performance in school. Throughout the years, controversies emerged about the measurement and utility of the construct, including concerns about the predictive validity of intelligence tests (Lewis, 1973), the role of nature versus nurture in determining intelligence (Kamin, 1974), and culture fairness of intelligence tests (Helms, 1997).

Robert Sternberg expanded the definition of *intelligence* to recognize that "the intelligent person is not one who merely does well on a test or in the classroom, but one who can use his or her mind to fullest advantage in all the various transactions of everyday life" (Sternberg, 1988, p. xiii). Thus, for Sternberg, "intelligence in everyday life is defined as the purposive adaptation to, selection of, and shaping of real-world environments relevant to one's life and abilities" (p. 65).

In the early 1990s, Peter Salovey and John Mayer expanded the notion of intelligence. They proposed a different type of intelligence that relies on affective input about the world, called *emotional intelligence*. They observed that individuals are both rational and emotional beings. Behaving successfully in life depends on the ability to respond to the environment both cognitively and emotionally. They proposed a set of skills that contribute to the accurate appraisal and expression of emotions, effective regulation of emotion, and use of feelings to motivate, plan, and achieve (Salovey & Mayer, 1990). Their framework for emotional intelligence includes four dimensions: (a) the ability to appraise and express emotional states, (b) the ability to use emotional states to facilitate thinking, (c) the ability to use information about emotions, and (d) the ability to regulate emotional responses (Salovey, Bedell, Detweiler, & Mayer, 2000). They suggested that differences in competency in using this affective information constitute emotional intelligence.

The case for expanding our understanding of intelligence to include the role of emotion has been popularized by Daniel Goleman. In his best-selling book, Goleman (1995) argued that emotional intelligence is as important as cognitive intelligence in determining behavior. Emotions such as anger, fear, happiness, surprise, and disgust have a powerful impact on behavior. He recounted situations in which people who are cognitively gifted perform poorly because their emotions interfere with situations, whereas people with average cognitive capabilities perform well because they are able to deal with their emotional response to a difficult situation. Relying on the earlier work by Salovey and Mayer (1990), Goleman (1995) defined five dimensions of emotional intelligence: (a) knowing one's emotions, (b) managing one's emotions, (c) motivating oneself, (d) recognizing emotions in others, and (e) handling relationships (p. 43).

Controversy about the definition, validity, and utility of this concept has been widespread (Barrett, Miguel, Tan, & Hurd, 2001). It has been argued that reliability and validity of measures of emotional intelligence have not been established, that the added contribution of emotional intelligence to cognitive ability tests for selection has not been demonstrated, and that Goleman's assertions about emotional intelligence are not supported with research data (Barrett et al., 2001).

Thus, although this topic may be appealing and has received much coverage in the popular press (Fisher, 1998; Goleman, 1998, 2000), emotional intelligence remains a controversial subject within the mainstream literature of psychology. To learn more about library research, this chapter focuses on the topic of emotional intelligence to illustrate the search for monographs. Using Goleman's (1995) book as a starting point, we search for other books that will help us understand emotional intelligence.

LIBRARY CATALOGS

To locate a book within the library's collection, we need an index to the collection. The library's catalog is that index. Until recently, for most libraries that index was the card catalog, a cabinet of drawers containing cards representing books in the library. Each card contained information that briefly described a book and enabled the user to locate that book in the library.

With increasing frequency, libraries are relying on machine-readable electronic computerized catalogs. As we proceed through this chapter, we discuss both the more traditional card catalog as well as the computer catalog.

We can begin to locate other information on emotional intelligence by starting with Goleman's (1995) book. Most libraries arrange books on their shelves by a code known as a *call number* printed on the spine (bound end) of the book. To find Goleman's book, we need to find its call number so that we can locate the book on the shelf. The index that provides this information is the catalog.

In the typical card catalog, as in most standard indexes, each book in the library has three types of cards in the catalog. There is a card for each author or editor of the book, a card for the title of the book, and a card for each major subject contained in the book. In an author index, information is arranged in alphabetical order by the last name of the person who wrote the book. In a title index, material is arranged alphabetically by the title of the book, ignoring initial articles *a, an,* and *the.* In a subject index, books are listed alphabetically by the subject or topic of the book. Table 4.1 illustrates each of these types of organizational schemes: author, title, and subject indexes. In some libraries these indexes are separated; in others they are combined.

When looking for a book by a particular person, we conduct an author search. Our author is Daniel Goleman. Because indexes organize author information alphabetically by the author's last name (surname), we search for *Goleman, Daniel.* Figure 4.1 provides an example of the catalog card for Daniel Goleman's book on emotional intelligence. Note that the author is listed at the top of the front card (1).

We also see in Figure 4.1 that the title of the book is *Emotional Intelligence* (2). It was published in New York, NY (3), by Bantam Books (4) in 1995 (5). Below this we find a physical description of the book (6): It contains 14 prefatory pages and 352 pages of text, it is illustrated, it is about 25 cm (9.3 in.) tall, and it contains references and an index. The International Standard Book Number (ISBN) (7) is a unique number assigned to this book by the publisher.

Below the descriptive information are the tracings (8). Tracings inform us how the book has been indexed and, in this case, include subject indexing information. A cataloging librarian who has examined the book assigns subject headings (tracings) that describe its contents. In this case, three subject headings have been assigned. Indicated by Arabic numbers, they are *Emotions, Emotions and cognition,* and *Emotions—Social aspects.* (Because the subjects identified in these tracings have been assigned to this book on emotional intelligence, we can reasonably assume that other books on emotional intelligence might also be identified by these subjects.) Based on this information, we can see that there are five ways to find this book in the catalog (five cards in the catalog): The book would be indexed alphabetically by the author (1), indexed by the title of the book (2a), and indexed by each of the three subject headings (8). (Additional tracings are

TABLE 4.1. Example of Alphabetical Ordering of Authors, Titles, and Subjects of Books

Author	Title	Subject
Adorno, T. W.	Basic behavioral statistics	Emotions
Allport, G. W.	Behavior and psychological man	Environment
Anastasi, A.	Behavior therapy	Evolution
Anderson, N. H.	The behavioral sciences today	Experiments
Aronson, E.	Being mentally ill	Fantasy
Bandura, A.	Beyond burnout	Fear

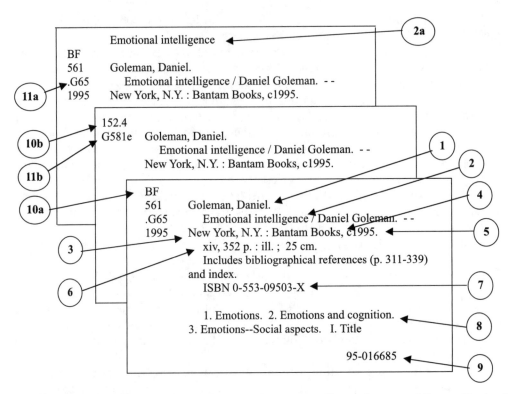

FIGURE 4.1. Examples of catalog cards for author entries illustrating use of Dewey Decimal and Library of Congress call numbers.

added for a book's coauthors or if the book is known by alternate titles, although this is not the case in this example.) The bottom line of the card contains the Library of Congress card number (9) for this book. This is a unique number to which librarians can refer in the process of ordering and cataloging books.

To find this book in the library, the most important piece of information you will need is the call number, typed in the upper left corner of the card. If your library uses the Library of Congress classification system, the call number is BF 561 .G65 1965 (10a), illustrated in the front card in Figure 4.1. If your library uses the Dewey Decimal Classification System, the call number is 152.4 G581e (10b), illustrated in the middle card in Figure 4.1. In most libraries you would go to the section of the library containing numbers similar to these to find the book. In some larger research libraries, you might have to place a written request for the book, use the call number, and have a library staff member retrieve the book.

CLASSIFICATION SYSTEMS

The Library of Congress and Dewey Decimal systems are the most widely used methods of organizing books in libraries in the United States. Several other systems do exist and may be found in specialized libraries (e.g., medical or agricultural libraries) or outside the United States.

The Dewey Decimal system was developed in the 1870s by Melvil Dewey to organize books in public and school libraries. Using 10 subject classes in three-digit numbers ranging from 001 to 999, which are then subdivided to represent more specific topics, the system was based on the state of knowledge at the time. For Dewey, 100 = Philosophy, 150 = Psychology (a branch of philosophy in the 1870s), 300 = Social Science, 610 = Medicine, and so forth. This system continues to be widely used by public libraries and some college libraries.

The Library of Congress classification system was developed in the late 1890s to organize collections in the Library of Congress, one of the largest libraries in the United States. The Library of Congress classification system uses a combination of letters and numbers to organize books by subject. Each entry begins with one or two letters representing a broad class of knowledge: for example, B = Philosophy, BF = Psychology, H = Social Sciences, R = Medicine, and so forth. These general areas are subdivided into narrower topics using numbers and letters.

Because there may be many books in the library on the same topic, the classification number is supplemented with a book number in both the Dewey Decimal and Library of Congress systems. For Goleman (1995), the book number in the Library of Congress system is .G65 (11a), and in the Dewey Decimal system it is G581e (11b). The most common book number system uses Cutter numbers. The Cutter number may be used to identify a subtopic for the book or to identify the author of the book; in some cases, two Cutter numbers may be used. In an edited book, with chapters written by different people, the Cutter number is often based on the book's title.

Thus each call number contains two parts: a classification number and a book number. In some cases, if the library has multiple editions of the same book, a date may be included in the call number to distinguish between editions. The result is a unique number for each book in the library; in Figure 4.1, this number is either BF 561 .G65 1995 (10a) or 152.4 G581e (10b).

In 1900, classification was believed to be very important. People wanted books organized so that volumes on related topics were located together on the shelf in the library. This would allow the user to not only find a particular volume in the catalog but also browse the shelves to find other related works. There are some fundamental curiosities related to these classification systems, based on their history and how the world was perceived at the time these systems were developed. For example, psychology is grouped as a subarea within philosophy (150 or BF), abnormal psychology is grouped within medicine (616 or RC), and educational psychology is grouped with education (370.15 or LB 1051). Therefore, psychology-related materials are scattered around a library under both Dewey Decimal and the Library of Congress classification systems, as illustrated in Table 4.2.

The location of materials in the library depends on judgments made by librarians who assign classification numbers and subjects to books. Librarians examining two similar books may make different decisions, books may contain more than one topic, or books may be written in emerging fields in which the terminology is in flux. For all of these reasons, seemingly related books may be assigned widely different classification numbers and thus be stored in different parts of the library.

Relying on the call number obtained from the catalog, we can find our book. Figure 4.2 (p. 45) shows where we can find Goleman's book relative to the call numbers of other books in our library. If we are using the Dewey Decimal system, our call number is 152.4 G581e. Note that the Dewey number moves from smallest to largest: 100 before

TABLE 4. 2. Distribution of Psychology-Relevant Materials in the Dewey Decimal Congress Classification Systems

Dewey Decimal	Subject area	Library of Congress
616.852–616.89	Abnormal psychology	RC512–RC571
158	Applied psychology	BF636–BF637
006.3	Artificial intelligence	Q334–Q336
155.4	Child psychology	BF721–BF723
153.4	Cognition	BF311
156	Comparative psychology	BF660–BF678
370.15	Educational psychology	LB1051–LB1091
620.82	Human factors	TA167
306.8	Family	HQ503–HQ1064
158.7	Industrial psychology	HF5548.8
153.8	Motivation	BF501–BF504
153.7	Perception	BF231–BF299
155.2	Personality	BF698
658.3	Personnel management	HF5549
152	Physiological psychology	QP351–QP495
362.2	Psychiatric social work	HV689
616.89	Psychotherapy	RC475–RC510
401.9	Psycholinguistics	BF455–BF463
519.5	Statistics (correlation)	QA278
150.151	Psychometrics	BF39–BF39.2
302	Social psychology	HM251–HM291
371.92	Special education	LC4601–LC4803

150 before 152 before 152.4 and so forth. Numbers representing the authors within the 152.4 class (C814, G222, G581e, G867) are ordered by letter (A, B, C, D, etc.) and within the same letter group as though preceded by a decimal point. If we are using the Library of Congress system, our call number is BF 561 .G65 1995. Note that B comes before BA comes before BF. BF13 is before BF311 before BF561. Within the BF561 class Cutter numbers for author are shelved by letter and within letters as though preceded by a decimal point (e.g., .B4, .E45, .G50, .G65, .G120, .H35). If there were multiple volumes with the call number BF 561 .G65, a date might be added (e.g., 1995, 1998).

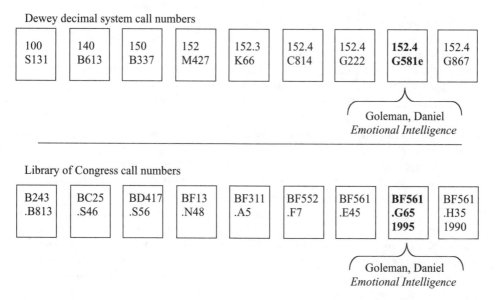

FIGURE 4.2. Location by call number of emotional intelligence book relative to call numbers of other books on the shelf.

SUBJECT HEADINGS

Recall that three subjects were assigned to Goleman's book when it was published and cataloged in 1995: Emotions, Emotions and cognition, and Emotions—Social aspects. Note that the term *emotional intelligence* was not assigned as a subject heading to describe this book. The topic of emotional intelligence was relatively new in the literature in 1995. (The authoritative source for the controlled vocabulary for subject headings used in most academic libraries in the United States is the Library of Congress Subject Headings.) The term was not added to the controlled vocabulary of Library of Congress Subject Headings until April 1999. As a result, the term would not have been assigned to any book on this topic before April 1999. If we conduct a subject search in a catalog using the subject heading emotional intelligence, we would find only books published after April 1999. We would have to use other related subject terms, such as *Emotions*, to attempt to find books on emotional intelligence published before April 1999. To know whether a term is included in the controlled vocabulary or when it was added to the controlled vocabulary, one would have to check a document such as the Library of Congress Subject Headings. For assistance, you might consult a reference librarian.

COMPUTER CATALOG

A growing number of libraries have eliminated the card catalog and instead rely on an online electronic catalog. Such electronic catalogs allow you to search the library's collection, as in the old card catalog, by looking for the author, title, or subject. However, there are advantages to newer electronic methods. In most cases, you are not limited by the controlled vocabulary of the subject index; you can also search on keywords (terms such as *emotional intelligence*) found in the subject headings, title, or other places in the record. You may also be able to limit the books in your search by language (Spanish only) or a period (items published after 1990). Using a Boolean structure as described in chapter 3, we can narrow a search's parameters.

The age of card catalogs brought consistency from library to library. Almost all libraries followed the rules and standards developed by national bodies such as the Library of Congress. Many libraries obtained their cards from just one or two sources (such as the Library of Congress), so even how the records looked was the same. However, electronic library catalogs introduced many differences in how records can be found and how they appear. In 2002 there were about a dozen different vendors providing computer catalog software to libraries (e.g., Dynix, Innovative Interfaces, and Voyager). Each electronic library catalog system has slightly different capabilities and behaves a bit differently. Libraries can often tailor the user interface software for their catalog systems to the needs of their own user populations; for example, some catalogs allow you to limit searches to those found in a particular location (e.g., reference books) or those housed in a separate library (e.g., a medical or business library). Of course, each library wants to have its own appearance and presentation to the public, especially for those people viewing the catalog remotely on the Web. In preparing this book we used electronic catalogs of many libraries, such as those of Cornell University, Lawrence University, Library of Congress, Marian College, Ripon College, University of Wisconsin-Milwaukee, and University of Wisconsin-Oshkosh, as well as the WISCAT catalog, which represents holdings for many libraries in Wisconsin. Each catalog is different from the others. In the discussion of computer catalogs that follows, we describe the use of a computerized library catalog in general conceptual terms. The figures illustrate the concepts of computer searching without the unique graphics for a particular library or software vendor. Recognize that as you use a library's computer catalog you will have to apply these general principles to the specific library catalog you are using. Let us start our computer search by assuming that we know of Daniel Goleman's book about emotional intelligence. How might we find this book using a computer catalog?

At the beginning, when we access the library's home page on the Web (whether we do it in the library or some other location) and we display the user interface, we may have to decide what to do. Do we want to learn about the library itself, its staff, hours, and collections? Do we want to search for articles in journals? In this case, we wish to use the online library catalog to locate books, so we will have to find a button or link to the library's online catalog. After we enter the library's online catalog, we will have to make a choice: How do we wish to search? Method 1, shown in Figure 4.3, asks us to specify from several options: author search, title search, subject search, and so on. An alternative approach, Method 2, suggests that we select from a basic search versus a guided search.

Suppose our library uses Method 1, and we want to locate the book by Daniel Goleman. We could decide to do an author search. As illustrated in Figure 4.4, we would specify the author's name (12).

The results of this search might be the one book. Figure 4.5 illustrates an example of the bibliographic record for the Goleman book. Note the similarity of this record to the catalog cards displayed in Figure 4.1. We find the record contains the same information about the author, title, publisher, description, bibliographic notes, subjects, Library of Congress card number, and call number (13). We also find a brief table of contents for the book (14); where it is located in the library (15); and the status "available" (16), meaning it has not been checked out of the library.

Method 1

Author	Keyword
Subject	Author & Title
Title	Call Number

Method 2

Basic Search	Search for the author, title, journal title, subject heading, or call number, or use a free text search to find items.
Guided Search	Use pull-down menus to construct your search to find items.

FIGURE 4.3. Two methods of selecting the type of online search.

12

Author Search

| Goleman, Daniel | **Search** |

Type the words you want to use in your search, and press <enter>, or click on Search.

FIGURE 4.4. Example of an author search.

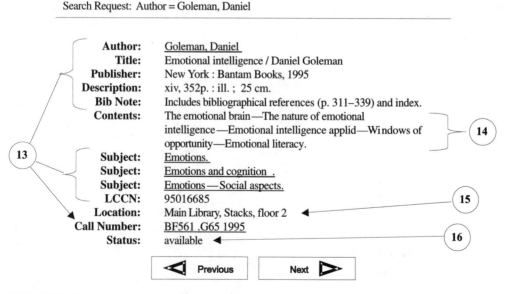

Search Request: Author = Goleman, Daniel

Author: Goleman, Daniel
Title: Emotional intelligence / Daniel Goleman
Publisher: New York : Bantam Books, 1995
Description: xiv, 352p. : ill. ; 25 cm.
Bib Note: Includes bibliographical references (p. 311–339) and index.
Contents: The emotional brain—The nature of emotional intelligence—Emotional intelligence applid—Windows of opportunity—Emotional literacy.
Subject: Emotions.
Subject: Emotions and cognition .
Subject: Emotions—Social aspects.
LCCN: 95016685
Location: Main Library, Stacks, floor 2
Call Number: BF561 .G65 1995
Status: available

13 **14** **15** **16**

Previous   Next

FIGURE 4.5. Example of an electronic bibliographic entry.

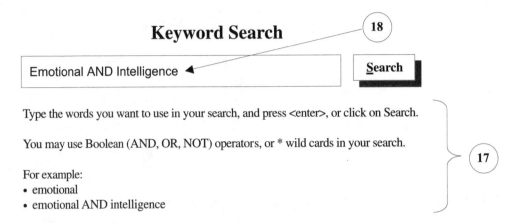

FIGURE 4.6. Example of a keyword search.

Using Method 1 (see Figure 4.3), suppose we choose a keyword search. We would find a user interface screen like that in Figure 4.6 Note that we have chosen to do a keyword search, not a subject search. The user interface screen provides some hints on structuring our search (17). Had we chosen a subject search, we would have scanned only the subject headings field. Because we used the term *emotional intelligence,* we would not have identified anything earlier than April 1999, when the term was added to the controlled vocabulary. By performing a keyword search, we will look for two terms, *emotional* and *intelligence,* in other fields such as the title field. Let us enter the terms *emotional* and *intelligence* (18), illustrated in Figure 4.6.

Suppose our library catalog used Method 2. If we asked for a basic search we might see a computer screen such as the one displayed in Figure 4.7. Here we select the type of search to conduct. We could decide to search by keyword or by author, title, call number, subject, journal title, or publisher name (19). (Some libraries offer other options.) We could also limit the search by elements such as English language (20), video

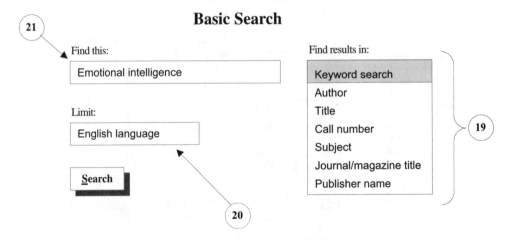

FIGURE 4.7. Example of a basic search.

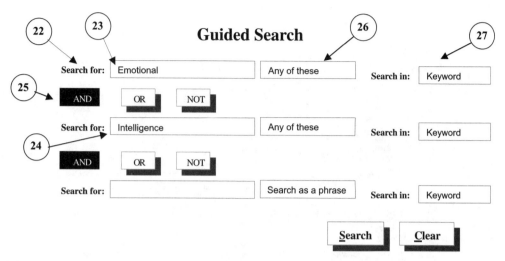

FIGURE 4.8. Example of a more complex search.

recording, or last 10 years. We have chosen to conduct a keyword search to specify the search terms emotional intelligence (21).

In a more complex search, such as a guided search, illustrated in Figure 4.8, we are able to exercise a bit more control over the search results. We have the ability to specify as many as three sets of search terms in the search field (22). In each space, we can specify one or several terms. We have indicated that the search must find the keywords *emotional* (23) and *intelligence* (24) somewhere in the record, using a Boolean **AND** (25) operator. For each set of terms in our search, we can decide whether we wish to search as a phrase (e.g., emotional intelligence; the two words must be adjacent), search for the words anywhere, or search to include all words (26). We can also independently specify the fields to search for each of the sets of terms: for example, author, title, subject, keyword, publisher, and date (27). In this case, we have asked to search the entire record for the terms *emotional* **AND** *intelligence,* using them as keywords.

Let us examine the results of our search. An example appears in Figure 4.9. At the top of the figure, we are reminded that we requested a keyword search using the terms *emotional* **AND** *intelligence* (28). Below this is a four-column table showing a brief listing of the first five records of materials in the library. For each record, we have a sequential number unique to this particular search (29), the full title of the document (30), the author (31), and the date of publication (32). Our list is ordered by publication date, starting with the most recent. (In many catalogs one can select the order in which citations are displayed.) In some records, because the work is an edited collection, there is no author listed in the author field (33). Some libraries may provide additional information on this results screen, such as location of the book in the library by floor, call number, and availability. As our screen displayed the first five records in our search, selecting the *Next* button (34) would display the next five records. (We have deleted many of the buttons and other graphics present in most online catalogs that direct you to common navigation options, such as those for starting a new search, directing you to another menu, sorting and display preferences, and viewing online hints.)

Let us take the next step and find out more about one of these books. The second item in our list on measurement of emotional intelligence looks interesting. Figure

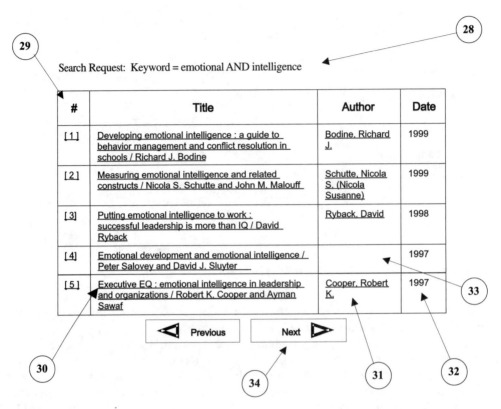

FIGURE 4.9. Example of the results of a search for books on emotional intelligence.

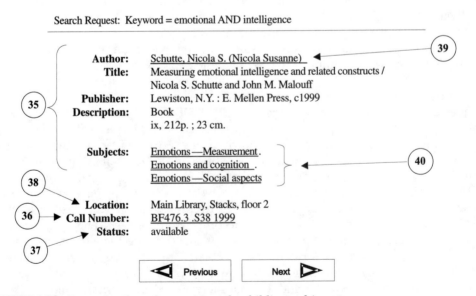

FIGURE 4.10. Example of an electronic catalog bibliographic entry.

4.10 shows an example of the possible appearance of the bibliographic record for the second item, the book on measurement of emotional intelligence by Nicola Schutte. Much as on a catalog card, we again see the author, title, publisher, description of the book, and subjects (35). The call number (36) enables us to find this book; because the book has a status of available (37), we should expect it to be located in the book stacks of our main library on the second floor (38). If the library whose catalog we were searching used the Dewey Decimal system for organizing its books, we would find a Dewey call number instead of the Library of Congress call number. Note the hyperlinked underscoring of the author's name (39) and each of the subject headings (40). Because these are hyperlinked, we could select any of these fields to conduct a new search, using each as the search term. In some catalogs, even more information might be provided. For some books, the table of contents is available; this is especially true for edited works such as handbooks and annual serials. In some cases, the Library of Congress catalog number or the ISBN may be provided. If we were using a unified catalog (e.g., WISCAT), including the contents of many different libraries, we would find information for each library that has the book and the call number in that library.

We should return to the list of records retrieved by our search and examine other records from the list in Figure 4.9, books by Bodine, Ryback, Salovey and Sluyter, and Cooper and Sawaf. We might advance to the next set of references retrieved. Then we might structure the search a bit differently to see if we can identify other sources. We probably have the ability to print a hard copy of the search or of the individual records. We can search the library shelves to find materials of interest. With some library catalogs you might have the option to save the electronic record or send a record to your e-mail address.

As you become experienced working with computer catalogs, you may encounter many complexities and subtleties to catalog searching that we have not addressed here. For example, an authority record will give you information about elements such as the subject headings themselves. Searching catalogs of large research collections, such as unified catalogs like Online Computer Library Center, OhioLINK, WISCAT, or the Library of Congress, that contain the holdings of many libraries, will often provide additional information. By pursuing these various sources, you can conduct a thorough search for monograph literature on your research topic.

REFERENCES

Barrett, G. V., Miguel, R. F., Tan, J. A., & Hurd, J. M. (2001, April). *Emotional intelligence: The Madison Avenue approach to science and professional practice.* Paper presented at the 16th Annual Meeting of the Society for Industrial and Organizational Psychology, San Diego, CA.

Fisher, A. (1998, October 26). Success secrets: A high emotional IQ. *Fortune,* 293–298.

Goleman, D. (1995). *Emotional intelligence.* New York: Bantam Books.

Goleman, D. (1998). What makes a leader? *Harvard Business Review, 76,* 92–102.

Goleman, D. (2000). Leadership that gets results. *Harvard Business Review, 78,* 78–90.

Helms, J. E. (1997). The triple quandary of race, culture, and social class in standardized cognitive ability testing. In D. P. Flanagan & J. L. Genshaft (Eds.), *Contemporary intellectual assessment: Theories, tests, and issues* (pp. 517–532). New York: Guilford Press.

Kamin, L. J. (1974). *The science and politics of IQ.* Potomac, MD: Erlbaum.

Lewis, M. (1973). Infant intelligence tests: Their use and misuse. *Human Development, 16,* 108–118.

Salovey, P., Bedell, B. T., Detweiler, J. B., & Mayer, J. D. (2000). Current directions in emotional intelligence research. In M. Lewis & J. M. Haviland-Jones (Eds.), *Handbook of emotions* (pp. 504–520). New York: Guilford Press.

Salovey, P., & Mayer, J. D. (1990). Emotional intelligence. *Imagination, Cognition, and Personality, 9,* 185–211.

Sternberg, R. J. (1988). *The triarchic mind: A new theory of human intelligence.* New York: Viking.

Terman, L. M. (1916). *The measurement of intelligence.* Boston: Houghton-Mifflin.

Thorndike, R. L., & Hagen, E. (1978). *The Cognitive Abilities Test.* Chicago: Riverside.

5 Psychology Journal Articles

Sources Discussed

American Psychological Association. APA PsycINFO. Retrieved January 10, 2002, from http://www.apa.org/psycinfo/

Psychological abstracts (1927–present). Washington, DC: American Psychological Association. Monthly.

Psychological index. (1894–1935). Washington, DC: American Psychological Association.

PsycINFO [computer database]. (1872–present). Washington, DC: American Psychological Association. Weekly.

Thesaurus of psychological index terms. (9th ed.). (2001). Washington, DC: American Psychological Association.

MOST PUBLISHED psychological research appears in the form of journal articles. There are many types of articles: for example, data-based research articles, review articles, theoretical articles, methodology articles, and editorials. Journals such as *Developmental Psychology, Journal of Applied Psychology, Journal of Personality and Social Psychology*, and *Learning and Memory* publish the results of research. Research articles follow the publication conventions contained in the *Publication Manual of the American Psychological Association* (APA, 2001) and use research approaches that a psychological research methods course and a textbook such as *Experimental Psychology* (Kantowitz, Roediger, & Elmes, 2001) might cover. A journal such as *Psychological Bulletin* publishes articles that summarize and evaluate the research in a particular area. The American Psychological Association's *Monitor on Psychology* is a magazine that provides information on current developments to association members. A journal such as *Psychology Today* does not present original research but summarizes research and topics for a lay audience. You will probably need to consult research journals, and a literature review contained in *Psychological Bulletin* could be useful. There are thousands of journals in psychology and related fields.

Quality of research publications is an important concern for psychologists. One method of ensuring quality of published research is the use of a peer review process. In a peer review system, when an article is submitted for publication, the journal editor sends the submitted article to a panel of experts in the area to determine its suitability for publication. Peer reviewers may consider factors such as whether the article offers new contributions, whether the methodology is sound, whether the data support the conclusions, and whether the article is clearly written. Reviewers make recommendations to the editor about the suitability of the article for publication and provide feedback to the author on changes that should be considered. Journals published by the American Psychological Association, the American Psychological Society, and other professional organizations use the peer review process to ensure quality of their publications. Some journals, however, do not use a peer review process. For such journals, you need to exercise extra caution to evaluate the quality of what you are reading.

Whereas you may have used indexes such as the *Reader's Guide to Periodical Literature* or *Periodical Abstracts* in high school to locate information, these are not adequate for your psychology research project because they do not cover most journals in psychology. PsycINFO and *Psychological Abstracts (PA)* are the most important sources of citations to research in psychology.

PsycINFO AND *PSYCHOLOGICAL ABSTRACTS*

PsycINFO is the most comprehensive indexing tool for identifying published literature of psychology. It contains citations and nonevaluative summaries of publications, is well indexed to allow a variety of search approaches, and is noteworthy for its breadth of subject coverage and the years it covers. It contains about 1.8 million entries as of 2002. It is also the database from which the monthly printed index, *PA*, is produced. *PA* began publication in 1927, and it was recognized for the depth of its indexing and long publishing history.

Fortunately for current researchers, recent PsycINFO enhancements provide excellent retrospective coverage of the discipline. Although PsycINFO began production in 1971, you can perform a retrospective search of all citations in *PA* back to 1927. PsycINFO also includes most of the contents of *Psychological Index*, the predecessor to *PA* that was published annually from 1894 to 1935. In addition, the database contains the contents of a series of bibliographies called the *Harvard Book Lists*, published at irregular intervals from 1938 to 1971.

PsycINFO provides all the features one might expect from a computer-assisted search: the ability to search for terms and phrases not included in the *Thesaurus of Psychological Index Terms,* including those in an abstract, and for terms or phrases in multiple fields and the ability to limit citations using strategies not possible in the printed indexes (by publication type, population or age group, publication format, journal in which an article was published, year of publication). An enhancement added in 2002 is the ability to view and search for references to published literature cited in each article or book chapter in the database. New citations appear in the database faster than is possible in the printed *PA*. Most database providers update their versions of PsycINFO files weekly, adding about 5,000 records per month, although a few provide monthly updates. Some search services allow you to save successful search strategies and run them at a later time. This feature permits you to update search results to include the most recent citations in the database.

The long publishing histories of *PA* and PsycINFO as well as changes in scholarly publishing have influenced the content and scope of publications each source includes. Early in the 20th century many of the publications indexed were intended for the generalist, and there were only a few journals that would now be considered scholarly material, that is, intended for the academic researcher or clinical practitioner. As the discipline of psychology matured and specialized branches of the field developed, the number of substantive, discipline-specific publications increased. PsycINFO currently indexes the following publication formats:

- Periodicals, articles, and annual review publications. At present, PsycINFO indexes approximately 1,900 serial publications published in dozens of languages from more than 50 countries. As of 2002, approximately three quarters of the citations in PsycINFO are to serial publications. In the case of foreign languages articles, the abstract is in English with a translated title, followed by the original title if it was published in a Roman alphabet. A separate field indicates the language of the original article. *PA* limits coverage to materials in English.

- Books and book chapters. For books that are edited volumes (that is, chapters by different authors that an editor compiles around a central theme), the book and each chapter are represented by a separate record in the database. There are citations to English-language titles only. Volumes in monograph series are also included: volumes published on a regular basis and containing subject-relevant articles. An example of the latter is *Monographs of the Society for Research in Child Development*.

- Doctoral dissertations. Although typically not published, dissertations are an important part of the research literature of psychology because they represent the result of original, scholarly activity. Subject-appropriate dissertations are selected from the publication *Dissertation Abstracts International, Part A* or *Part B* (see chapter 10 for detailed information about *Dissertation Abstracts International*). *PA* does not include citations to dissertations after 1980.

- Research or technical reports. These include reports produced by research institutes (e.g., Department of Psychology at the University of South Africa), government agencies (e.g., U.S. Air Force Research Laboratory), and professional associations (e.g., American Psychological Association Research Office). Coverage of research reports in PsycINFO is selective.

- Letters, errata and corrections, editorials, and obituaries. These items are most often published in journals but are not articles as such. However, they can contain important information because they comment or expand on previously published material or correct material that appeared in tables, figures, or the text of an article.

Several categories of publications are not included in PsycINFO. For example, until 2002, this index did not include book reviews, and it does not include what are considered news articles (as in *Monitor on Psychology*).

The coverage and scope of both products (printed and database) have changed over time. More than 800 journals and 1,200 books, dissertations, and other materials were reviewed for possible inclusion from 1969 to 1971. In 1981 approximately 1,000 journals were regularly scanned. By 1988 that number had increased to more than 1,400 titles, and in 2002 the journal coverage list had expanded to more than 1,900 titles in dozens of languages. The journals from which articles are selected for *PA* and PsycINFO are not limited to psychology publications. PsycINFO indexers review hundreds of journals in related disciplines, such as biology, education, management, medicine, psychiatry, social work, and sociology, and include those articles related to psychology in the database. At the same time, there is more consistent coverage of nonjournal material, such as books and book chapters. Figure 5.1 illustrates the growth of references in the PsycINFO database.

Number of Entries

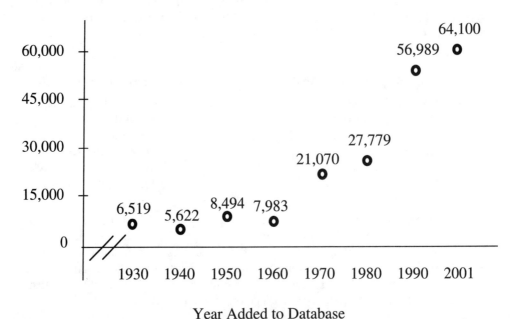

FIGURE 5.1. Number of Citations represented in the PsycINFO Database by publication year of citations (E. Welsh, personal communication, September 30, 2002).

Before describing the mechanics of doing a search, we describe a topic in psychology to illustrate that search process, focusing on the psychology of the self.

CHAPTER EXAMPLE: GENDER DIFFERENCES IN SELF-DEFINITION

What is the self? It includes thoughts and beliefs about ourselves as well as an awareness of who we are. We started by consulting the *Handbook of Social Psychology*. A chapter by Baumeister (1998) described the self in terms of three components: reflexive consciousness, interpersonal being, and executive function. Reflexive consciousness is the experience of awareness of our own thoughts and actions. Interpersonal being involves the social interactions we have with others that define our relationships. The executive function is the decision maker and controller, the part of us that directs behavior. The person is aware of self. We exist in relation to others, and the self is defined in part by those relationships. The self develops over time and takes responsibility for self-regulation.

There are many facets of self. For example, self-awareness is used to describe the experience of attending to oneself. Self-esteem refers to the extent to which a person's evaluation of his or her self is positive. Self-presentation refers to the ways in which we engage in social interactions as a function of what we disclose of ourselves as others are watching. Self-efficacy refers to the extent to which people believe they can exert control over their environment. Self-regulation enables the capacity to change. These and other aspects of self described by Baumeister (1998) demonstrate the rich nature of self as a psychological concept.

How does gender affect self-definition? Maccoby (1990) indicated that gender differences are most pronounced in social situations. Behavior is situational and appears to differ based on the composition and size of the social group in which the individual is functioning. Cross and Madson (1997b) argued that women in the United States are more likely to have an interdependent view of themselves and that men are more likely to have an independent view of themselves. Maccoby reported that American girls are more likely to develop intimate friendships and focus on social relationships and that boys are more likely to engage in activities involving competition and dominance. Boys tend to play in larger groups and in public places, and their play takes up more space; girls are more likely to play in yards or homes. Baumeister and Sommer (1997) stated that adult women tend to focus more on cooperation and intimacy with a small number of persons; men are more likely to have relationships with a large number of others, and those relationships focus on power and status.

The topic of gender differences in self-definition has been widely researched and reported in the literature of psychology. This chapter focuses on gender differences in self-definition to illustrate the search for journal research literature in psychology. Using Maccoby (1990) and Baumeister and Sommer (1997) as a starting point, we can search for other articles that could help us to understand this topic better.

USING PsycINFO

One can take several approaches to searching PsycINFO. If you have identified a few key citations that are highly relevant to the topic, the attributes of those citations can be used to locate similar, highly relevant citations. Another approach is to use key terms and phrases representing your topic's search strategy (discussed in chapters 2 and 3) to conduct a subject or keyword search.

Our example assumes we have identified several highly relevant citations to the journal literature. We can begin our search by finding those references. We examine the records representing them in PsycINFO and use elements of those records to search for others.

Field-Restricted Author Search

Beginning with the Baumeister and Sommer (1997) article we can use a field-restricted approach to searching; that is, we can control which fields of the database we wish to search, for example, title, author, abstract, subject headings, journal title, and so forth. Here we limit our search to the author fields of the records and restrict output to items published in a particular year in order to locate the citation for this article. In a hard-copy index, this is comparable to doing an author search in a particular year's index. The search is structured as shown in Figure 5.2. We have specified a search limited to the author (AU) field of the database (1), looking for the names Baumeister and Sommer (2), and we have restricted our search to materials published in the year 1997 (3). Our search yielded several citations, one of which is our target article, "What Do Men Want? Gender Differences and Two Spheres of Belongingness," in *Psychological Bulletin*. Viewing the PsycINFO record in Figure 5.3, we see three types of information.

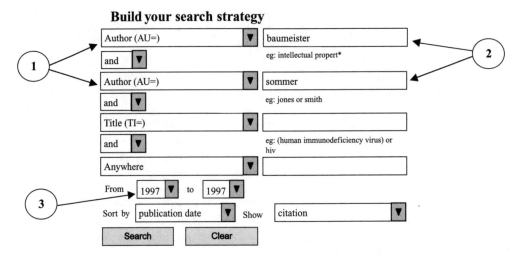

Build your search strategy

FIGURE 5.2. Example of a PsycINFO field-restricted search using two author names in 1997. From PsycINFO database, copyright Cambridge Scientific Abstracts. Reprinted by permission.

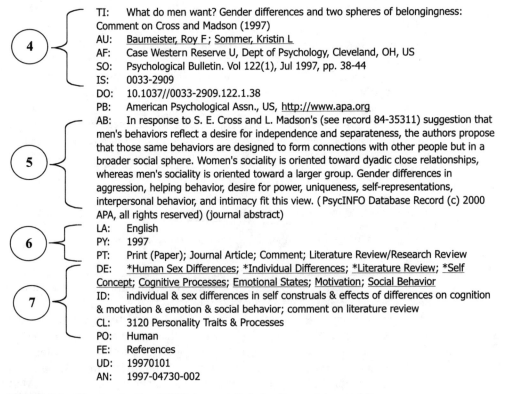

FIGURE 5.3. Citation in PsycINFO to an article by Baumeister and Sommer.

Bibliographic information (4) identifies basic publication information. These elements include the title of the article (TI), followed by names of the authors (AU) and the institutional affiliation of the first author (AF). (Beginning in 2002, citations added to the database include the affiliations of all authors. More recent PsycINFO citations than the one in Figure 5.3 include e-mail and mailing addresses for the author designated to respond to questions about the article.) Following this is publication information, including the journal in which the article was published (SO), with year, month, volume, issue number, pages on which the article appeared, and International Standard Serial Number (ISSN). The ISSN is a unique code that distinguishes this journal from all others. There is a brief abstract (AB) summarizing the article's content (5). The content of the abstract is often the same as in the abstract preceding the published article, although PsycINFO may revise it to enhance computer retrieval. This abstract was prepared by the authors and appeared in the journal. It was published in English (LA) in the year (PY) 1997 (6). There is also information about the subject content of the article (7).

The Subject Approach

The subject headings (7) displayed in the PsycINFO record provide information that is useful for locating additional citations on your topic. PsycINFO indexers select and assign subject headings, called descriptors (DE), from the *Thesaurus of Psychological Index Terms* to represent the content of this article. *Thesaurus* subject headings are designated as major and minor, reflecting the emphasis the indexers believe are the primary and secondary focus of the article; major descriptors are indicated by an asterisk. (We detail methods for using the *Thesaurus* later in this chapter.) A key concepts or identifier (ID) field provides additional descriptive information and is helpful because it often contains words or phrases that reflect the content of the article but that may not be in the structured vocabulary of the *Thesaurus* or in the article's abstract. The classification (CL) is indicative of a conceptually broad subject area in which this publication has been grouped. These broad categories, such as Personality Psychology (code 3100), are also subdivided into narrow subcategories, for example, Personality Traits & Processes (3120). These categories change over time. They are also used to organize the printed *PA* issues; therefore, consult a current monthly *PA* issue for an up-to-date list of the categories, or see the PsycINFO Web site.

By reviewing the title, abstract, *Thesaurus* subject descriptors, and key phrases assigned to articles identified in the process of defining the topic (e.g., Baumeister & Sommer, 1997; Cross & Madson, 1997b; Maccoby, 1990) we can begin to compile a list of terms and formulate a search that will locate other relevant citations. After reviewing several such citations reflecting our topic we can compile a table of terms or phrases that reflect each concept similar to that illustrated in Figure 5.4. We have constructed a search that includes three primary concepts: gender differences, self-concept, and social interaction. For each concept we have identified search terms that might be used to represent the concept. To conduct a search, we use these terms and variations of them to search for additional document citations as illustrated in Figure 5.5. We have specified a search using Keywords (KW) (8). In the Cambridge Scientific Abstracts search interface for PsycINFO shown in Figure 5.5, the KW option search includes the title (TI), subject headings (DE), and key concepts (ID) fields. We have also used a Boolean structure for our search (9). The search can be represented as *(gender difference* **OR** sex role*)* **AND** *(self-*

Concept	Search terms
Gender differences	Gender differences
	Sex roles
Self-concept	Self-esteem
	Self-confidence
	Self-concept
	Self-definition
Social interaction	Social behavior
	Social interaction
	Social environment

FIGURE 5.4. Search terms and phrases.

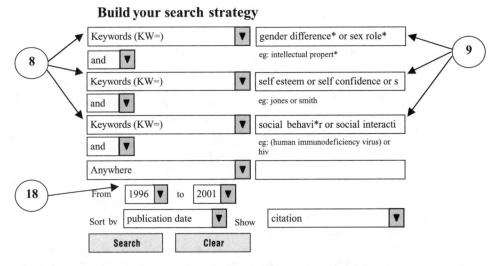

FIGURE 5.5. Example of a keyword search using Cambridge Scientific Abstracts interface to PsycINFO. Search consists of KW = (gender difference* **OR** sex role*) **AND** KW = (self-esteem **OR** self-confidence **OR** self-concept **OR** self-definition) **AND** KW = (social behavi*r **OR** social interaction* **OR** social environments). From PsycINFO database, copyright Cambridge Scientific Abstracts. Reprinted by permission.

esteem **OR** *self-confidence* **OR** *self-concept* **OR** *self-definition)* **AND** *(social behavi*r* **OR** *social interaction*** **OR** *social environment*).*

Because PsycINFO and vendors of the PsycINFO database, such as Cambridge Scientific Abstracts, allow truncation and wild-card capabilities (discussed in chapter 3) in searching, we can use these features to accommodate plural forms of words with variant spellings, as demonstrated in this search. For example, *sex role** retrieves the phrases *sex role* and *sex roles; behavi*r* finds both the American *behavior* and the English/Canadian *behaviour.* Truncation can also be used in author searches, especially if an author varies how his or her name appears in publication. Truncation and wild cards should be used with care because they may have unintended consequences for your search results. Using wild cards can lead to retrieval of many unwanted citations. For example, *india** retrieves

India, Indians, and *Indiana.* Using truncation and wild cards for common words in psychology also results in a large number of citations; for example, *behav** will retrieve any of the following terms: *behavior, behaving, behaviors,* and *behavioral.*

Figures 5.6 and 5.7 contain citations retrieved with our search strategy. The first, in Figure 5.6, is an article appearing in *Sex Roles,* which is concerned with the impact of social context. As in prior examples, the entry includes bibliographic information, such as the article title (TI), authors (AU), and source (SO) journal (10). It also includes the article abstract (11), subject descriptors, and other information (12) that describes the content and format of the study. The subject population (PO) on which this study is based has been identified (13).

The second source, identified in Figure 5.7, describes a book chapter titled "Development of the Self in Gendered Contexts" (14), written by Bettina Hannover (15). It was published on pages 177–206 in a book edited by Thomas Eckes and Hanns Trautner, *The Developmental Social Psychology of Gender* (16). A lengthy abstract (AB) summarizing the article is provided (17). (Some search services provide hyperlinks for book and chapter records that link all chapters to the records for the books in which they were published.)

These records can give us ideas about how to narrow search results if the number of citations retrieved is too large. One idea is to limit the number of years searched. Note that our search illustrated in Figure 5.5 restricted citations to those published in journals from 1996 to 2001 (18). PsycINFO records also contain publication- or content-type codes (PT) that allow you to narrow a search to books, chapters, journal articles, dissertations, or reports (19). Content codes can limit searches to specific types of publications (for example, case study, literature/research review, empirical study). You can limit your results by population (13), such as human or animal, male or female, or age group; language of publication (20); or broad classification categories (21) reflecting the subject areas used to organize citations in *PA.* (The order and format in which these elements

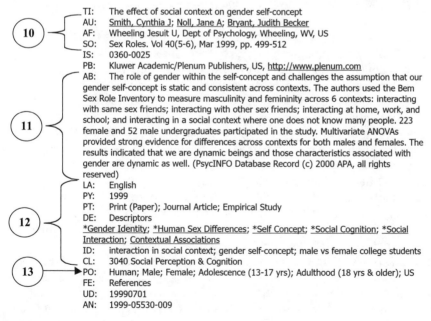

FIGURE 5.6. Example of a journal article entry in PsycINFO. Fron PsycINFO database, copyright Cambridge Scientific Abstracts. Reprinted by permission.

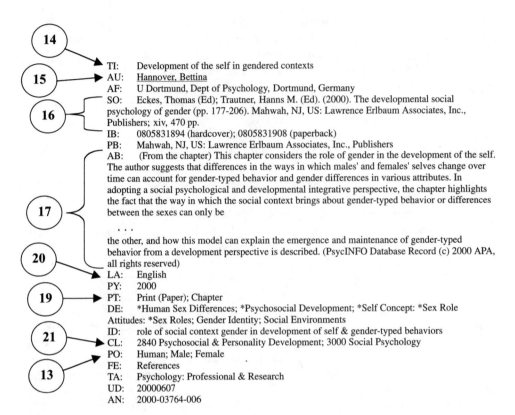

TI: Development of the self in gendered contexts
AU: Hannover, Bettina
AF: U Dortmund, Dept of Psychology, Dortmund, Germany
SO: Eckes, Thomas (Ed); Trautner, Hanns M. (Ed). (2000). The developmental social psychology of gender (pp. 177-206). Mahwah, NJ, US: Lawrence Erlbaum Associates, Inc., Publishers; xiv, 470 pp.
IB: 0805831894 (hardcover); 0805831908 (paperback)
PB: Mahwah, NJ, US: Lawrence Erlbaum Associates, Inc., Publishers
AB: (From the chapter) This chapter considers the role of gender in the development of the self. The author suggests that differences in the ways in which males' and females' selves change over time can account for gender-typed behavior and gender differences in various attributes. In adopting a social psychological and developmental integrative perspective, the chapter highlights the fact that the way in which the social context brings about gender-typed behavior or differences between the sexes can only be

       . . .

       the other, and how this model can explain the emergence and maintenance of gender-typed behavior from a development perspective is described. (PsycINFO Database Record (c) 2000 APA, all rights reserved)
LA: English
PY: 2000
PT: Print (Paper); Chapter
DE: *Human Sex Differences; *Psychosocial Development; *Self Concept: *Sex Role Attitudes: *Sex Roles; Gender Identity; Social Environments
ID: role of social context gender in development of self & gender-typed behaviors
CL: 2840 Psychosocial & Personality Development; 3000 Social Psychology
PO: Human; Male; Female
FE: References
TA: Psychology: Professional & Research
UD: 20000607
AN: 2000-03764-006

FIGURE 5.7. Example of a citation to a book chapter in PsycINFO. From PsycINFO database, copyright Cambridge Scientific Abstracts. Reprinted by permission.

appear, how they are searched, and what they are called vary among database services. The PsycINFO Web site contains a guide to the contents of records, and each online service describes the organization of records on its site.) Using these features to tailor your search has many advantages and some drawbacks. As noted in chapter 3, the more restrictions you place on a search, the greater the chances that you will miss citations that are relevant to your topic. If you are seeking research that uses a particular type of research methodology (for example, a case study), using a publication-type restriction might be useful. Searching for a subject population of chimpanzees might be useful to a comparative psychologist.

On the other hand, we might focus on a journal. If we found several highly relevant articles in a particular journal, we could focus on that journal. For example, several relevant articles appeared in *Sex Roles*; therefore, it is reasonable to assume that there might be other related articles. We could construct a search limited to this particular publication in the journal source title field.

Several side notes are in order. First, a discussion of theory may appear in print from several perspectives. The Baumeister and Sommer (1997b) article in volume 177, issue 1 of *Psychological Bulletin* and another commentary written by Martin and Ruble (1997) were in response to earlier work by Cross and Madson (1997a). Additionally, there was an accompanying response to these two comments by Cross and Madson. Second, we began our search by studying a handbook chapter. Third, in contrast to these review articles, work retrieved from *Sex Roles* provides results of research. Your research may require familiarity with both review and research articles.

Thesaurus Search

With a completely different approach, we can expand our PsycINFO keyword search by consulting the *Thesaurus of Psychological Index Terms*. We might rely on keywords identified in the process of defining and narrowing our topic in chapter 2 and illustrated in a sample computer search in chapter 3. By consulting the *Thesaurus*, we may find terms to refine our search. Consulting a thesaurus, or controlled vocabulary, has some advantages over using only those terms you discover on your own. By using standardized terms assigned by PsycINFO indexers, you do not have to think of all possible variations of phrases reflecting you topic. The *Thesaurus* can also be helpful for finding terms that are related to one another, including some that you may not have considered in your preliminary review of the topic. Keep in mind, however, that it takes time before terms commonly used by authors in the discipline are selected and included in the *Thesaurus*. Also, the topic you are investigating may be fairly new and have little established, commonly accepted terminology. In this case, searching for terms in titles, abstracts, or key phrases may be required.

You can use the printed volume, although most databases provide access to the *Thesaurus* as part of their PsycINFO subscription. Both the print and online versions have three components. We start by searching with the *Thesaurus* option (22), as illustrated in Figure 5.8, for the term *gender differences* (23).

The result of our *Thesaurus* search illustrated in Figure 5.9 indicates that the term *gender differences* is not used as a subject heading. The acceptable term for this concept, indicated by the Use Instead reference (24), is *Human Sex Differences*, which has additional terms listed under it. *Gender differences* was used as a subject heading until 1973, information that

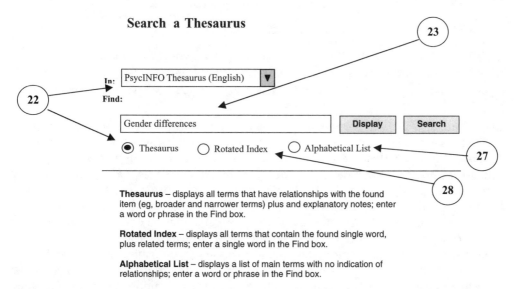

FIGURE 5.8. Searching the online *Thesaurus of Psychological Index Terms*. From PsycINFO database, copyright Cambridge Scientific Abstracts. Reprinted by permission.

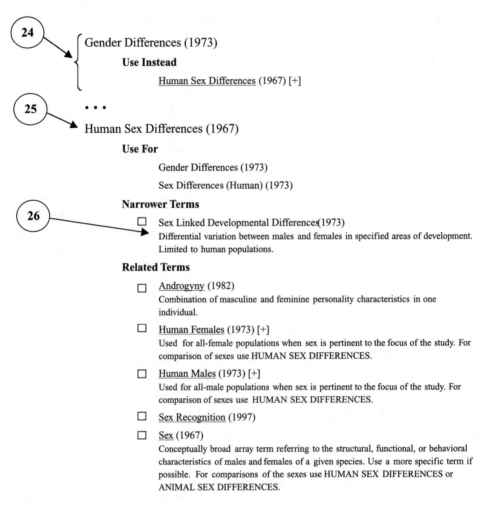

FIGURE 5.9. Entries from the *Thesaurus* resulting from searching the phrase "gender differences" and the corresponding entry for the term "Human Sex Differences." From the PsycINFO database, copyright Cambridge Scientific Abstracts." Reprinted by permission.

may be useful when you use the older printed *PA* subject indexes. Note that throughout PsycINFO and the *Thesaurus* certain words or phrases are underlined, indicating hyperlinks that refer you to another part of the database. By clicking on the Human Sex Differences link, we are referred to another part of the *Thesaurus* where we see that the term has been used as a subject heading since 1967 (25). It is also used in place of the terms Gender Differences and Sex Differences (Human). The *Thesaurus* also refers us to conceptually narrower terms and related terms that we might consider adding to our list of subject terms. (Some *Thesaurus* entries also refer us to conceptually broader terms, although none are indicated for Human Sex Differences.) Some terms are accompanied by a scope note, or precise definition of the term as it is used in the controlled vocabulary and assigned to citations in PsycINFO. These notes are helpful for differentiating among terms that are similar and defining terms that may be commonly misused or misunderstood. An example is the definition of Sex-Linked Developmental Differences (26) in Figure 5.9.

The Alphabetical List (27) search option, noted in Figure 5.8, is a variation of the *Thesaurus* search. This list locates all terms (those that are and are not part of the controlled vocabulary) in alphabetical order. Clicking on the hyperlink shown in Figure 5.9 for the displayed terms provides the related, narrower, broader use for, and scope note information described earlier.

Another approach is to use the Rotated Index (28) seen in Figure 5.8 (p. 63). Unlike the previous approach, this feature allows you to find a word in whatever position it appears in the *Thesaurus*, whether as a stand-alone term or as part of a phrase. Figure 5.10 shows the results of a search for the word *roles* in the Rotated Index. The resulting list contains not only *Roles* but also *Gender Roles* (29) and *Sex Roles* (30). The see reference and scope note (31) inform us that Sex Roles is used instead of Gender Roles as an indexing term within PsycINFO and *PA*.

In most cases using a combination of keyword and *Thesaurus* terms is a good strategy when conducting a subject search in PsycINFO. *Thesaurus* terms, however, were not compiled and applied to PsycINFO citations before 1967. Therefore, a search seeking publications added to the database before 1967 cannot rely on terms from the *Thesaurus*.

Using Information in the Cited References List

A second way to find articles related to those you find in a database is to examine the publications used by the authors, that is, those works cited in the reference lists. This can be accomplished by using citations retrieved in a PsycINFO search.

In 2002 PsycINFO added the ability to view and search cited references. Cited references (CR) are attached to all records added to the database after 2000, and the CR field appears for some publications as early as 1988. In contrast, an indexing tool that was

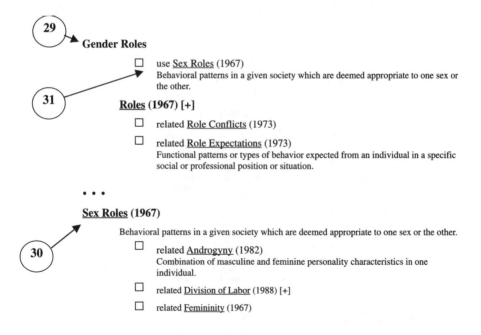

FIGURE 5.10. Entries from the *Thesaurus* Rotated Index. From the PsycINFO database, copyright Cambridge Scientific Abstracts. Reprinted by permission.

originally constructed to take advantage of cited reference searching, *Social Sciences Citation Index (SSCI)*, provides extensive retrospective coverage of more journal publications from all social science disciplines. See chapter 7 for an extended discussion of the premise of citation searching and how to use *SSCI*.

Earlier in this chapter we discussed an article by Baumeister and Sommer (1997) and used it to illustrate a PsycINFO entry in Figure 5.3. An updated version of Figure 5.3 is provided in Figure 5.11, illustrating some of the information added with the 2002 PsycINFO. Note that the name of the author [Baumeister], related to the affiliation (AF), has been added (32). The label (Print) indicates that this is the ISSN for the hard-copy version of this journal. Most citations in PsycINFO as of 2002 do not provide cited references; however, the NR field indicates the number of references cited by the authors (33) when this information is available. Note that the total number of references in the article is 41, although only 40 are listed as part of this citation. Citations that are not published (such as correspondence received by the authors, information received in personal interviews, or citations in non-Roman languages) are not included in the cited references in PsycINFO. This is followed by the first few of the 40 references to published literature cited by the authors (34). The Cambridge Scientific Abstracts interface used in the Figure 5.11 example allows you to go directly from a cited reference in the list to the PsycINFO record for the item, if one exists. In addition, you can view references in the PsycINFO database that also cited each reference as well as other PsycINFO entries that cite this article (that is, the Baumeister and Sommer article).

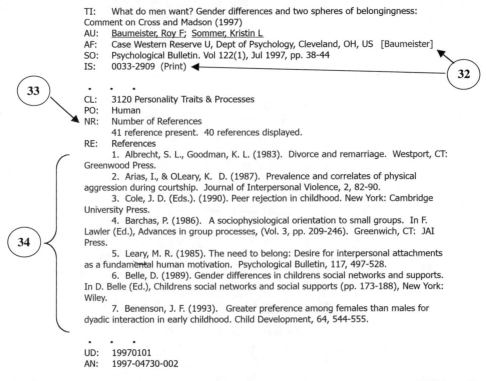

FIGURE 5.11. Citation in PsycINFO to an article by Baumeister and Sommer (1997). From the PsycINFO database, copyright Cambridge Scientific Abstracts. Reprinted by permission.

USING *PSYCHOLOGICAL ABSTRACTS*

Had we used *PA* (the printed index) instead of PsycINFO, we would have found some similar information. It might have been more difficult, however, to locate the information as we would have been limited to searching by author and subject. Knowing of the Baumeister and Sommer (1997) article, we could consult the volume 84 (1997) *PA* Author Index to locate the citation. A small portion of the Author Index, displaying the author entries for our article, is shown in Figure 5.12. We would have found entries for both the first author Baumeister (35) and the second author Sommer (36). Under the first author's name (35) we find the full citation for the article (37) and an entry number indicating that this is entry 35304 in volume 84 of *PA* (38). Note that under the second author's name the entry number is provided (38) but the citation is not provided; instead we are referred back to the entry for the first author for the citation with a *See* reference (39).

Had we chosen to search by subject we would have found this article indexed in several places in the *PA* Subject Index to volume 84. This article appears in the Subject index under four different subject headings shown in Figure 5.13: Human Sex Differences (40), Individual Differences (41), Literature Review (42), and Self Concept (43). Note that these four subject headings are the major descriptors (DE) identified with an asterisk (*) in the electronic entry shown in Figure 5.3 (7). The other descriptors

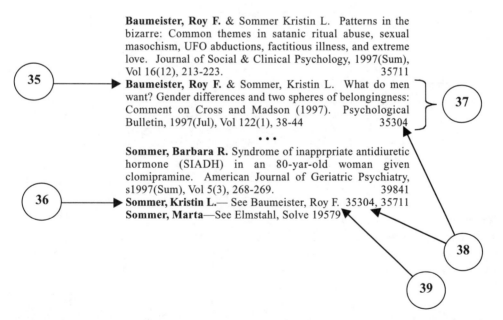

Volume 84
AUTHOR INDEX

Baumeister, Roy F. & Sommer Kristin L. Patterns in the bizarre: Common themes in satanic ritual abuse, sexual masochism, UFO abductions, factitious illness, and extreme love. Journal of Social & Clinical Psychology, 1997(Sum), Vol 16(12), 213-223.   35711
Baumeister, Roy F. & Sommer, Kristin L. What do men want? Gender differences and two spheres of belongingness: Comment on Cross and Madson (1997). Psychological Bulletin, 1997(Jul), Vol 122(1), 38-44   35304

• • •

Sommer, Barbara R. Syndrome of inapprpriate antidiuretic hormone (SIADH) in an 80-yar-old woman given clomipramine. American Journal of Geriatric Psychiatry, s1997(Sum), Vol 5(3), 268-269.   39841
Sommer, Kristin L.— See Baumeister, Roy F. 35304, 35711
Sommer, Marta—See Elmstahl, Solve 19579

FIGURE 5.12. Example of Author Index entries for Baumeister and Sommer (1997) article in printed *Psychological Abstracts*. Reprinted with permission of the American Psychological Association, publisher of *Psychological Abstracts* and the PsycINFO® Database (Copyright 1872–present by the American Psychological Association). All rights reserved.

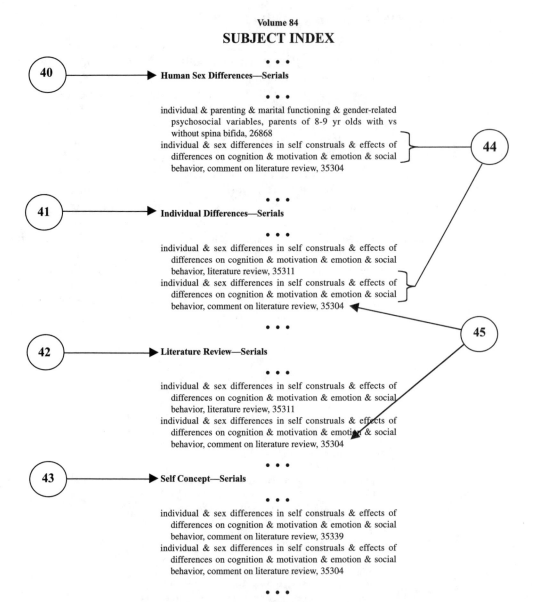

FIGURE 5.13. Examples of Subject Index entries for Baumeister and Sommer (1997) article in printed *Psychological Abstracts*. Reprinted with permission of the American Psychological Association, publisher of *Psychological Abstracts* and the PsycINFO® Database (Copyright 1872–present by the American Psychological Association). All rights reserved.

attached to this citation in the database (Cognitive Processes, Emotional States, Motivation, and Social Behavior) are not used as indexing terms in *PA* as these concepts are considered a secondary focus of the article. In each entry we have a brief description of the subject content of the article: "individual & sex differences in self construals & effects of differences on cognition & motivation & emotion & social behavior, comment on literature review" (44). This is the identifier (ID) attached to the article in the PsycINFO database. The number 35304 (45) is the entry number for this particular citation in volume 84 of *PA*. Turning to entry 35304 we would find a bit more information. Entry 35304 is displayed in Figure 5.14. as it appeared in the October 1997 issue of *PA*. In addition to the full citation for the article (46) we have information about the affiliation of the first author (47) and the abstract of the article (48) that appeared in the journal. As noted earlier, several things are not included in *PA*. PsycINFO information about this article that is not included in *PA* includes the list of subject headings attached to this article, subject population, and ISSN.

ACCESS TO PsycINFO

Today, few libraries rely solely on the printed *PA*. Begun in 1971, the PsycINFO database was one of the first bibliographic databases made available for online searching. Before user-friendly search interfaces were developed, searches were limited to experienced online users (mostly librarians). There are now a variety of options for searching PsycINFO. Ask a reference librarian for information about what bibliographic systems are available on your campus and for assistance in using them.

Who provides access to PsycINFO? Several vendors provided online access as of spring 2002. The American Psychological Association (APA), the producer of PsycINFO, provides access through the APA Web site. Throughout this chapter examples have been based on the search interface provided to PsycINFO by Cambridge Scientific Abstracts. SilverPlatter provides access to PsycINFO, one of dozens of databases available through its WebSPIRS search interface. FirstSearch, provided by the Online College Library Center (OCLC), makes PsycINFO available as one of its online database products. ProQuest Information and Learning, a subsidiary of Bell & Howell, also makes available a version of PsycINFO. A complete and current list of vendors is available on the PsycINFO Web site.

PERSONALITY PSYCHOLOGY

• • •

47

35304. **Baumeister, Roy F. & Sommer, Kristin L.** (Case Western Reserve U, Dept of Psyuchology, Cleveland, OH) **What do men want? Gender differences and two spheres of belongingness: Comment on Cross and Madson** (1997). *Psychological Bulletin*, 1997(Jul), Vol. 122(1), 38-44.—In response to S. E. Cross and L. Madson's (see record 84-35311) suggestion that men's behaviors reflect a desire for independence and separateness, the authors propose that those same behaviors are designed to form connections with other people but in a broader social sphere. Women's sociality is oriented toward dyadic close relationships, whereas men's sociality is oriented toward a larger group. Gender differences in aggression, helping behavior, desire for power, uniqueness, self-representations, interpersonal behavior, and intimacy fit this view. —*Journal abstract*

46

48

• • •

FIGURE 5.14. Example of main entry for Baumeister and Sommer (1997) article in printed *Psychological Abstracts.* Reprinted with permission of the American Psychological Association, publisher of *Psychological Abstracts* and the PsycINFO® Database (Copyright 1872–present by the American Psychological Association). All rights reserved.

Although the content of PsycINFO is consistent across vendors, search capabilities, display options, appearance of records, and other features differ. Consulting help screens, tutorials offered online by the provider, or information that your library makes available will help you understand the unique capabilities of the particular version of PsycINFO you are using. The PsycINFO Web site also provides helpful search guides on the capabilities and search features of each system. Unless you personally pay a fee directly to one of these services and become an online subscriber, your access to PsycINFO will be through the interface provided by your college or university library. Because of the cost of the service, most libraries subscribe to only one version of PsycINFO. Become familiar with the one available through your college or university library. In some cases you may have remote Web access to your library's version of PsycINFO from your home or dormitory room, connecting through the library's Web page. Remote access may require a user ID and password to log on; if this is the case, consult a librarian for assistance.

If your campus does not have access to the PsycINFO file or if using it is inconvenient for you (for example, during semester breaks when you are away from campus), there are several "pay as you go" services that allow individuals to subscribe to database access. Jascó (2001) describes a few such services; a current list of providers is available on the PsycINFO Web site. Intended for students and professionals, these services charge by the number of searches conducted or citations retrieved, or they offer unlimited searching on a flat fee basis.

Electronic Document Retrieval

Online electronic access to research journals is becoming increasingly widespread. Several significant sources of electronic psychology journals exist. There are two ways in which you can access them.

The first approach is for libraries to subscribe to titles the same way they subscribe to printed ones. Instead of finding issues shelved in the library, you can link to a journal title directly from an entry in the online catalog. An example of such a service is PsycARTICLES, produced by the APA, which provides the full text of articles from journals published by the APA, the Canadian Psychological Association (CPA), the Educational Publishing Foundation (EPF), and an additional set of journals from Hogrefe and Huber (H&H) Publishers. As of 2002 coverage from 1988 to the present is provided for 50 psychology journals, such as *Developmental Psychology* (APA), *Neuropsychology* (APA), *Psychology of Addictive Behaviors* (EPF), *Canadian Journal of Experimental Psychology* (CPA), and *European Psychologist* (H&H). Some PsycINFO database vendors offer access to PsycARTICLES as part of their own services; it can also be offered in conjunction with PsycINFO. In these cases, citations in PsycINFO are linked to complete articles in PsycARTICLES where they exist, and the articles can be displayed in HTML format for viewing or printing. Thus, you can locate particular articles by conducting a PsycINFO search linked to the PsycARTICLES database.

The second approach is by linking to the full text of an article from its citation in a bibliographic database. Several vendors (such as EBSCO, OCLC, Ovid, and SilverPlatter) that provide access to the PsycINFO database provide access to PsycARTICLES titles in this way. If you identify a relevant citation when searching PsycINFO, there may be a link to the complete article. A similar service is ProQuest Psychology Journals, which provides full text for approximately 300 journals in psychology (for the most part, a different set of titles than PsycARTICLES). Coverage varies by the journal: some start as early as 1988 (e.g., *Adolescence* and *Crime and Delinquency*); others start as recently as 2000 (e.g., *Behaviour*

Change and *Canadian Journal of Occupational Therapy*). To locate a relevant journal article for viewing or printing, you search the ProQuest Psychology Journals version of the PsycINFO database and access full-text articles.

It is important to keep in mind that widespread availability of full-text journal titles is a relatively new development. Not all journal publishers make their titles available in electronic format to individuals or libraries. Of those that do, some make only the most current years of their journals available. For example, *Psychological Bulletin* is available electronically from PsycARTICLES beginning with the 1988 issues, but the journal began publication in 1904. For now, if you are seeking an important article published in a 1971 issue of the *Journal of Applied Psychology,* you must retrieve it in either hard copy or microform. Finally, your campus library may choose not to add all electronic journals to their collection. Publishers often require additional fees beyond the cost of paper subscriptions for access to their electronic equivalents, making the additional access expensive for many libraries. You should be cautious about relying solely on electronic publications when using research journals. Remember that ignoring a citation to a highly relevant article because it is not readily available in machine-readable form may result in your missing a key source for your paper.

e-psyche

This competitive product, e-psyche, indexes serial literature focusing on psychology and psychology-related articles in related disciplines. Beginning with production in 2000, e-psyche plans to index approximately 3,600 periodical publications (Kuranz, 2002). It includes citations to dissertations and Web sites and currently adds about 4,500 citations per month. It bears many similarities to PsycINFO; for example, much of the content of records is similar to PsycINFO, and e-psyche has its own thesaurus. As of late 2002, e-psyche's advantages include indexing of Web-based material and coverage of a range of nonacademic publications. It also promises to provide greater coverage of nonclinical areas of psychology. The greatest shortcoming of e-psyche is years of coverage. It currently includes citations only from 1998 to the present, although this coverage is expected to expand. Robertson (2001) also suggested that a sizeable percentage of periodicals indexed by e-psyche is not refereed. Given recent changes in PsycINFO, such as reference searching and expanded retrospective coverage, it will be interesting to watch the progress of e-psyche.

A FINAL NOTE ON PSYCHOLOGY JOURNAL INFORMATION

As you have noticed, the world of information is changing. PsycINFO has undergone significant changes, one being the addition of cited references to the most recent citations in the file. Electronic sources of psychology journal articles are available now that did not exist a few years ago, and their availability and years of coverage continue to expand. Coverage provided by services mentioned in this chapter continue to change. Whereas the print version of *PA* once provided primary access to psychological literature, PsycINFO now does so. In *PA* you can search by author and subject and retrieve a journal abstract, but you need to pay careful attention to the *Thesaurus* to validate search terms. PsycINFO contains all of the features of *PA* and offers much more: a keyword search, abstract search, linking to full text of some articles, and so forth. The ability to search many years or to construct a Boolean search makes PsycINFO a more efficient and effective alternative to printed indexes.

In this chapter we have attempted to illustrate general principles of searching for relevant psychology journal articles. We hope that these general principles will not change too radically. What will change is the content of databases, who makes databases available, what journals are covered, how the information is presented to users, and how you access this information.

REFERENCES

American Psychological Association. (2001). *Publication manual of the American Psychological Association* (5th ed.). Washington, DC: Author.

Baumeister, R. F. (1998). The self. In D. Gilbert, S. Fiske, & G. Lindzey, (Eds.). *The handbook of social psychology.* (4th ed., Vol. 2, pp. 680–740). New York: McGraw-Hill.

Baumeister, R. F., & Sommer, K. L. (1997). What do men want? Gender differences and two spheres of belongingness: Comment on Cross and Madson (1997). *Psychological Bulletin, 122,* 38–44.

Cross, S. E., & Madson, L. (1997a). Elaboration of models of the self: Reply to Baumeister and Sommer (1997) and Martin and Ruble (1997). *Psychological Bulletin, 122,* 51–55.

Cross, S. E., & Madson, L. (1997b). Models of the self: Self-construals and gender. *Psychological Bulletin, 122,* 5–37.

Jascó, P. (2001). Savvy searching. *Online Information Review, 25,* 62–65.

Kantowitz, B. H., Roediger, H. L., & Elmes, D. G. (2001). *Experimental psychology: Understanding psychological research.* Belmont, CA: Wadsworth.

Kuranz, J. (2002, May). e-psyche: Mission, facts, features & future. *Online-Mitteilungen, 73.* Retrieved August 12, 2002, from http://www.uibk.ac.at/sci-org/voeb/om/om73_kuranz.pdf

Maccoby, E. E. (1990). Gender and relationships: A developmental account. *American Psychologist, 45,* 513–520.

Martin, C. L., & Ruble, D. N. (1997). A developmental perspective of self-construals and sex differences: Comment on Cross and Madson (1997). *Psychological Bulletin, 122,* 45–50.

Robertson, M. (2001). E-psyche: A comparison of content with PsycINFO. *Behavioral and Social Sciences Librarian, 20*(1), 1–13.

6 Psychology-Related Sources

MANY PROBLEMS that psychologists study are complex and multifaceted. Whereas some questions are specific to psychology, others may be posed from a variety of viewpoints by researchers in related fields such as sociology or social work, education, life sciences, psychiatry, and business. People educated in different disciplines investigate some of these questions, and research is conducted on some problems in a multidisciplinary fashion. As researchers report their findings in their own professional fields, bodies of literature are built on related aspects of a topic in many different journals, conferences, and publications.

Many areas of psychology regularly intersect with other disciplines. For example, educational psychologists often report work relevant to educators, and research literature in education may be relevant to the educational psychologist. Literature and reports on management and business problems may be relevant to the industrial, organizational, engineering, or consumer psychologist. Abnormal and social psychologists may need to refer to the literature in sociology or social work. Physiological, clinical, and comparative psychologists may find literature in the health sciences relevant. Psychological researchers who do not consult this related literature may overlook important findings and theoretical approaches.

Although PsycINFO and *Psychological Abstracts (PA)* provide the most important entrée to psychological literature, indexing and abstracting services in related fields are of potential interest to psychologists. This chapter illustrates the use of several sources in fields related to psychology. The chapter is divided into four sections, presenting sources that provide access to literature in education, management and business, health sciences and psychiatry, and sociology.

We begin by focusing on the general topic of stress. We selected stress because it is an example of a problem that has been investigated by researchers across disciplines. Aspects of this problem have been examined from many perspectives. As we discuss each discipline, we use a particular aspect of stress to illustrate the search in a discipline using the bibliographic sources of that discipline.

CHAPTER EXAMPLE: STRESS

What is stress? In an early description of stress, Walter Cannon (1932) described the body's general reaction to stress as the fight-or-flight response. That is, when exposed to threat, the body prepares itself for one of two possible responses, either to stand and fight or to run away.

Two decades later, endocrinologist and physician Hans Selye (1956) provided an explanation for stress that he called the "general adaptation syndrome." Published in his classic work, *The Stress of Life*, this explanation of stress as a nonspecific response of the body to any demand was based on many years of observation and research about what Selye called the clinical syndrome of just being sick. The general adaptation syndrome has three phases. The initial response to a stressor is an alarm reaction. Second is the stage of resistance, when the body is exposed to continued stress and for a time adapts to the stressful condition. Third, after prolonged exposure, is the stage of exhaustion.

Kozicz and Casey (1999) noted that stress had been conceptualized from both physiological and psychological perspectives. Physiological stress was well defined by Selye (1956). Lazarus and Folkman (1984) focused on the cognitive appraisal component of psychological stress. It is the individual's interpretation of the environment as hostile that elicits the stress response. Primary appraisal occurs when one perceives the threat. Stress occurs when the individual's resources do not seem to be adequate to cope with the environmental threat. Secondary appraisal takes place as the individual evaluates what can be done to reduce the threat and identifies coping options and available resources (Lazarus, 1966). Because individuals are different, their responses vary.

Many responses to stress occur. Short-term, immediate responses to stress involve the autonomic nervous system, musculoskeletal system, and psychoneuroendocrine system. Specific responses include changes in arterial blood pressure, renal blood flow, heart rate, cholesterol, secretion of catecholamine and cortisol, release of epinephrine, muscle tension, and muscular rigidity (Goldberger & Breznitz, 1982; Kozicz & Casey, 1999; Steptoe & Appels, 1989). Longer term prolonged stress has been linked to coronary heart disease, arteriosclerosis, cardiac arrhythmia, depression, anger and aggression, ulcers, headaches, and sleep disorders (Goldberger & Breznitz, 1982; Kozicz & Casey, 1999; Steptoe & Appels, 1989).

Research has been conducted on many aspects of stress, and numerous books and articles have been written. As we focus on specific sources in fields related to psychology, we identify examples of specific aspects of stress in that literature that are of potential interest to psychologists: test anxiety in education, travel stress in management, coronary heart disease in health sciences, and alienation in sociology.

EDUCATION

Sources Discussed

Ask ERIC. (1992–present). Syracuse, NY: ERIC Clearinghouse on Information & Technology, Information Institute of Syracuse, Syracuse University. Retrieved March 15, 2002, from http://www.askeric.org/

Current index to journals in education. (1969–present). Washington, DC: U.S. Department of Education, National Library of Education, Educational Resources Information Center (ERIC).

Education index. (1929–present). New York: H. W. Wilson.

Resources in education. (1966–present). Washington, DC: U.S. Department of Education, National Library of Education, Educational Resources Information Center (ERIC). Formerly *Research in education*.

Thesaurus of ERIC descriptors. (14th ed.). (2001). Washington, DC: Educational Resources Information Center (ERIC).

Section Example: Test Anxiety

Evaluation situations occur frequently and to many persons. They occur in many contexts, such as evaluation in school, interviewing for a job, and appearing in court. Test anxiety is a particular case of a stress response in a performance-evaluation situation. Individuals with a high level of anxiety may be concerned about possible failure in an evaluation context (Sieber, 1980). People who experience test anxiety may exhibit sub-optimal test performance that masks their true knowledge or ability. Robert Sternberg (1996) began *Successful Intelligence* by describing his early response to intelligence tests. He reports the following:

> I failed miserably on the IQ tests I had to take. I was incredibly test anxious. Just the sight of the school psychologist coming into the classroom to give a group IQ test sent me into a wild panic attack. And by the time the psycholo-gist said, "Go!" to get us started, I was in such a funk that I could hardly answer any of the test items. . . For me, the game of taking the test was all but over before it even started. (p. 17)

What is test anxiety? Beidel, Turner, and Taylor-Ferreira (1999) defined test anx-iety as "an extreme fear of performing poorly on examinations" (p. 630). To the extent that we are not prepared or feel that we are not performing well in a situation in which our performance is being assessed, we may feel extremely uncomfortable, that is, under stress. This discomfort may interfere with our ability to think and perform. According to Angus McDonald, test anxiety is a "specific form of a wider group of problems charac-terized by feelings of 'anxiety.'" It is "primarily a concern over negative evaluation" (McDonald, 2001, p. 90).

There is considerable concern about educational evaluation and tests (McDonald, 2001). Test anxiety appears to correlate with task difficulty (Sarason, 1980). It appears to interfere with performance on cognitive tasks (Sarason, 1984). In the fol-lowing section, to illustrate a search in education, we focus on test anxiety in an educa-tional context as one aspect of stress. What mediates test anxiety? Are there ways to reduce test anxiety?

Education Sources

The two primary providers of bibliographic access to materials in education are the Educational Resources Information Center (ERIC) and H. W. Wilson Company.

Educational Resources Information Center

Established in 1966 by the U.S. Office of Education, the Educational Resources Information Center (ERIC) is supported by the U.S. Department of Education Office of Educational Research and Improvement. ERIC's initial purpose was to provide access to unpublished documents produced as a result of education-related government programs and grants. Since 1966 the scope and activities of ERIC have expanded to include cover-age of journals and other materials.

The ERIC database contains approximately 1 million abstracts of documents and journal articles on education. ERIC provides several important services to researchers needing information about education. The primary sources offered are *Resources in Education (RIE)* and *Current Index to Journals in Education (CIJE).*

For access to unpublished conference proceedings, position papers, research reports, curriculum guides, doctoral dissertations, and other materials, you can turn to *RIE*, formerly *Research in Education. RIE* is updated monthly. The documents cited in *RIE* can be purchased from the ERIC Document Reproduction Service, which can provide more than 50,000 documents electronically and most others in hard-copy or microfiche formats. For years the ERIC Document Microfiche Collection has provided copies of ERIC *RIE* documents to more than 800 (mostly college and university) libraries in the United States and Canada in the form of microfiche.

Access to journals is provided by *CIJE*, which covers approximately 980 journals in education and related disciplines. Most entries include a brief abstract of article contents. The *Thesaurus of ERIC Descriptors* provides the controlled vocabulary of subject search terms for *RIE* and *CIJE.*

RIE and *CIJE* are available in both hard-copy and electronic form. The electronic versions of *RIE* and *CIJE* are available in CD-ROM, on the Internet, and from several service providers, such as Ask ERIC and SilverPlatter.

Wilson Education Database

A second significant provider of access to materials in education is the H. W. Wilson Company, publisher of *Education Index (EI).* Initiated in 1929, *EI* is published monthly and cumulated annually and provides access to English-language materials on education. As of 2001 *EI* provided coverage of more than 525 core periodicals, monographs, and yearbooks in education. Education Database, also from H. W. Wilson, includes all of the content in *EI* and is available in electronic form as a CD-ROM, online through WilsonWeb, and other sources. Wilson initiated *Education Abstracts* to supplement indexing of journals with abstracts of the journal articles, with coverage starting in 1994. Education Full Text includes the full text of many journal articles in electronic form (either full-image PDF or HTML), starting with June 1983. Both *Education Abstracts* and Education Full Text are included in Wilson's Education Database.

Wilson's Education Database has several advantages over the ERIC family of products. Education Database and *EI* are useful for searching education journal literature published before 1969, when ERIC initiated *CIJE.* Access to the full text of many journal articles is also an advantage of Education Database.

EI has several disadvantages compared with the ERIC system. The coverage of *EI* is much less broad than that of *CIJE*, including about half the number of journals. Abstracts are not available for articles covered in *EI* and were not available in Wilson's online service until 1994. *EI* does not provide access to the many unpublished materials included in *RIE.* Because of the cost of these services your library may provide access to only one of them. Identify which one is available, and learn to use it.

ERIC Literature Search

To find information on test anxiety among college students, we turn first to ERIC. We use two concepts, test anxiety and college student, and link these with Boolean **AND** for an intersection. For ease and efficiency of searching we use an electronic database. Let us start with an example using the Internet Ask ERIC public access version of the database, available at http://www.askeric.org/

After selecting and entering our ERIC database, we see a search screen that might look something like the online version of Ask ERIC, presented in Figure 6.1. (Keep in mind that each search service displays information on the search screens differently, and services may ask different questions. Additionally, the screens that you see today may be different than the ones we had available as we wrote this book.) We enter two terms and because each is a multiword concept (e.g., 'test anxiety'), we enclose the phrase in single quotation marks, consistent with the requirements of this site's search software (1). We also specify that these are keywords (2). This directs the search software how to query the database; it examines multiple fields including subject, title, and abstract. Had we specified that a term was of author type, it would only search the author field in the database; had we specified title as the type, it would only search the title field of records. Also note that we have structured a Boolean intersection linking keywords with **AND** (3). A citation is retrieved only if it contains both sets of terms. Although we could limit our search to only journal articles (4) by selecting the journal articles check box, we have chosen not to do so, and we may find unpublished documents within our search results. Additionally, although we could limit our search to a particular time (5), for example, between 1995 and 2000, or since 1998, we have chosen not to do this. When satisfied that we have defined the search appropriately we submit our request to begin searching the ERIC database.

The computer displays a new screen showing the results of the search in a brief form. Figure 6.2 illustrates a portion of that list of results, and our search strategy is summarized at the top of the list (6). The search identified a total of 11 citations that satisfied the parameters of the search. For each item we see a relevancy score (7), indicating how closely it matches the search parameters (1000 is a perfect match, and 0 is totally

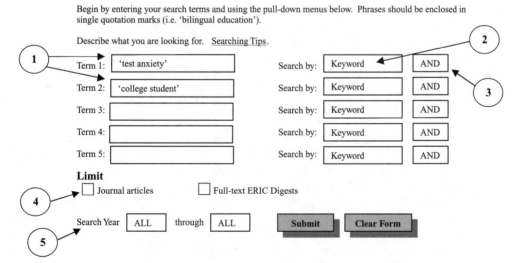

FIGURE 6.1. Example of an ERIC search on text anxiety. Initial screen, using "Ask ERIC" on-line.

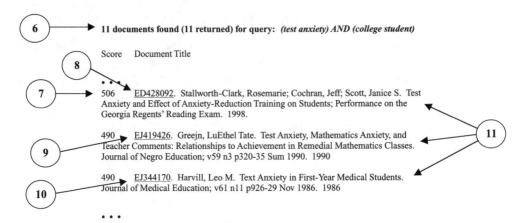

FIGURE 6.2. List of citations returned in an ERIC search on text anxiety using "Ask ERIC."

unrelated). There is a unique ERIC identifying number (8) for each item. Identification numbers that begin with an ED are ERIC Documents and are included in *RIE*. Item ED428092 (8) is a document that appears in the *RIE* print index and is in the form of an unpublished research report. Numbers beginning with EJ represent journal articles that are included in *CIJE*. The other two items in Figure 6.2, EJ419426 (9) and EJ344170 (10), are journal articles that are indexed in *CIJE*. Additionally, we see the citation for each item retrieved (11).

Note that the identifying number for each citation in the list is underlined (hyperlinked), indicating a link to another part of the database. Selecting hyperlinked citation number ED428092 (8), we see a new screen that provides the full *RIE* entry for this document, as illustrated in Figure 6.3. The entry begins with the document number (8), followed by the title (12), author (13), and publication date (14). The full abstract that appeared in the document is included (15). The *Thesaurus of ERIC Descriptors* is the controlled vocabulary (or subject heading list) for ERIC, and the *Thesaurus* terms assigned to this item are included in the Descriptors field (16). Identifiers (17) are terms that are not chosen from the *Thesaurus* but that provide additional information about the content of this document. This is a brief document, 11 pages in length (18). The document is available from EDRS (19) for a fee, although if your library has an EDRS collection it may be available in your library. The article is in English (20) and was originally presented as a conference paper (21). This abstract appears in hard-copy form in the July 1999 issue of *RIE* (22).

To illustrate differences between search services, we next turn to the EBSCO Host version of ERIC. EBSCO is an aggregator, a company that provides a service offering online Web access to many databases in a variety of disciplines. Although we are searching only the ERIC database here, one of the interesting attributes of aggregators such as EBSCO is that one may be able to search multiple databases at the same time. As illustrated in Figure 6.4 (see p. 80) we have entered the EBSCO Host version of the ERIC database and decided to do an advanced search. We have specified our search terms (23) and the fields (24) to be searched (author, title, etc.) and have linked these search parameters with Boolean operators (25) to create an intersection. We are also able to provide additional information to clarify our search. We might choose to limit our search to items that appear in Full Text within the database (26), if there were no access to interlibrary loan

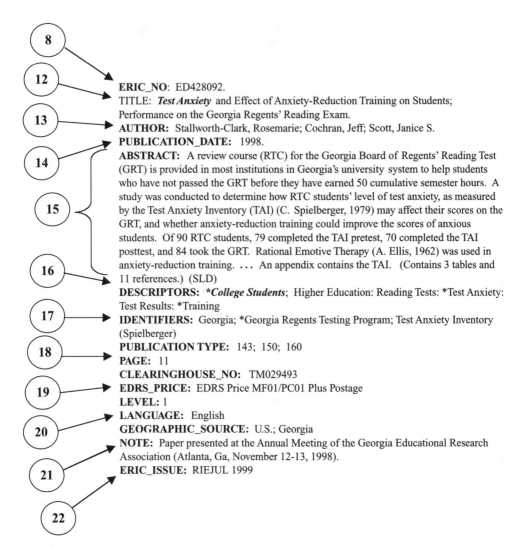

8

12

13

14

15

16

17

18

19

20

21

22

ERIC_NO: ED428092.
TITLE: *Test Anxiety* and Effect of Anxiety-Reduction Training on Students;
Performance on the Georgia Regents' Reading Exam.
AUTHOR: Stallworth-Clark, Rosemarie; Cochran, Jeff; Scott, Janice S.
PUBLICATION_DATE: 1998.
ABSTRACT: A review course (RTC) for the Georgia Board of Regents' Reading Test
(GRT) is provided in most institutions in Georgia's university system to help students
who have not passed the GRT before they have earned 50 cumulative semester hours. A
study was conducted to determine how RTC students' level of test anxiety, as measured
by the Test Anxiety Inventory (TAI) (C. Spielberger, 1979) may affect their scores on the
GRT, and whether anxiety-reduction training could improve the scores of anxious
students. Of 90 RTC students, 79 completed the TAI pretest, 70 completed the TAI
posttest, and 84 took the GRT. Rational Emotive Therapy (A. Ellis, 1962) was used in
anxiety-reduction training. ... An appendix contains the TAI. (Contains 3 tables and
11 references.) (SLD)
DESCRIPTORS: *College Students; Higher Education: Reading Tests: *Test Anxiety:
Test Results: *Training
IDENTIFIERS: Georgia; *Georgia Regents Testing Program; Test Anxiety Inventory
(Spielberger)
PUBLICATION TYPE: 143; 150; 160
PAGE: 11
CLEARINGHOUSE_NO: TM029493
EDRS_PRICE: EDRS Price MF01/PC01 Plus Postage
LEVEL: 1
LANGUAGE: English
GEOGRAPHIC_SOURCE: U.S.; Georgia
NOTE: Paper presented at the Annual Meeting of the Georgia Educational Research
Association (Atlanta, Ga, November 12-13, 1998).
ERIC_ISSUE: RIEJUL 1999

FIGURE 6.3. Sample *RIE* document resume from an ERIC search on text anxiety using
"Ask ERIC."

(see chapter 11), or we have only a very short time to complete our project. We could also
limit searching to a particular journal (27) or specify a time frame (28). Additionally, we
could qualify our search using particular fields within each record, such as country of
publication or language.

The results of this search are different from those of the prior search; we have
identified only eight sources in the database that satisfy all parameters of the search.
Figure 6.5 provides an example of the first three of eight sources identified. Let us take a
look at the full entry for the first item in our list, "Multicomponent Treatment of a Test
Anxious College Student" (29), journal article EJ591229 (30), by selecting the hyperlinked article title.

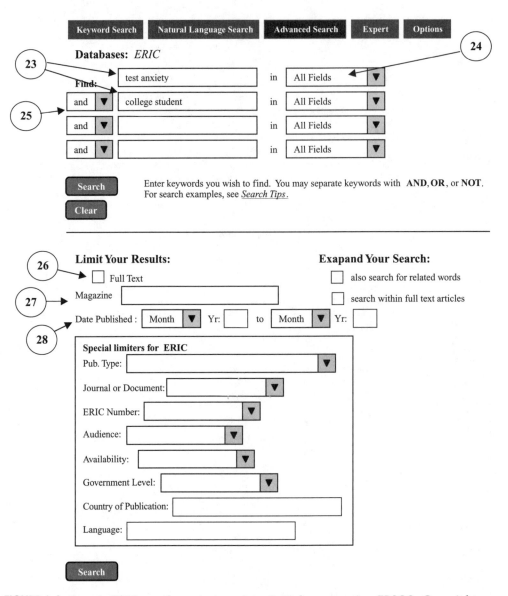

FIGURE 6.4. Sample ERIC search on text anxiety. Initial screen using EBSCO. Copyright, EBSCO Publishing, 2002. All rights reserved. Reprinted by permission.

The complete indexing entry for this journal article on test anxiety (29), EJ591229 (30), is illustrated in Figure 6.6. Many of the information fields contained in this journal abstract are similar to fields for a document report, but there are two important differences. The full bibliographic citation for the article source is provided (31): It appeared on pages 203–217 of the May 17, 1999 (volume 22, issue 2), edition of the journal *Education and Treatment of Children*. Additionally, we are provided with the International Standard Serial Number (ISSN), 07488491, a unique number assigned to this publication to differentiate it from any other magazine or journal that may have the

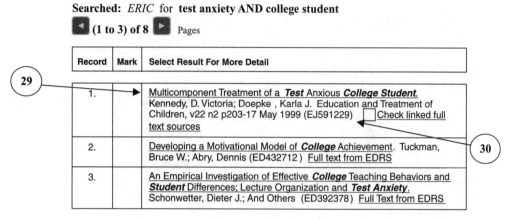

Record	Mark	Select Result For More Detail
1.		Multicomponent Treatment of a **Test** Anxious **College Student**. Kennedy, D. Victoria; Doepke , Karla J. Education and Treatment of Children, v22 n2 p203-17 May 1999 (EJ591229) ☐ Check linked full text sources
2.		Developing a Motivational Model of **College** Achievement. Tuckman, Bruce W.; Abry, Dennis (ED432712) Full text from EDRS
3.		An Empirical Investigation of Effective **College** Teaching Behaviors and **Student** Differences; Lecture Organization and **Test Anxiety**. Schonwetter, Dieter J.; And Others (ED392378) Full Text from EDRS

FIGURE 6.5. Sample results of an ERIC search for articles on test anxiety using EBSCO. Copyright, EBSCO Publishing, 2002. All rights reserved. Reprinted by permission.

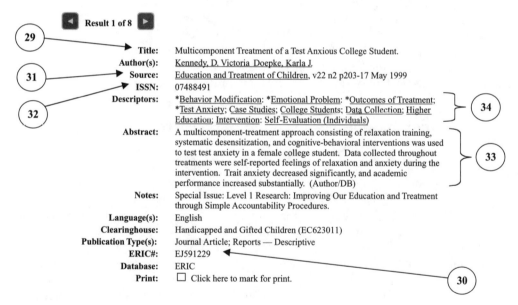

◀ **Result 1 of 8** ▶

Title:	Multicomponent Treatment of a Test Anxious College Student.
Author(s):	Kennedy, D. Victoria Doepke, Karla J.
Source:	Education and Treatment of Children, v22 n2 p203-17 May 1999
ISSN:	07488491
Descriptors:	*Behavior Modification; *Emotional Problem; *Outcomes of Treatment; *Test Anxiety; Case Studies; College Students; Data Collection; Higher Education; Intervention; Self-Evaluation (Individuals)
Abstract:	A multicomponent-treatment approach consisting of relaxation training, systematic desensitization, and cognitive-behavioral interventions was used to test test anxiety in a female college student. Data collected throughout treatments were self-reported feelings of relaxation and anxiety during the intervention. Trait anxiety decreased significantly, and academic performance increased substantially. (Author/DB)
Notes:	Special Issue: Level 1 Research: Improving Our Education and Treatment through Simple Accountability Procedures.
Language(s):	English
Clearinghouse:	Handicapped and Gifted Children (EC623011)
Publication Type(s):	Journal Article; Reports — Descriptive
ERIC#:	EJ591229
Database:	ERIC
Print:	☐ Click here to mark for print.

FIGURE 6.6. Sample *CIJE* journal article entry from an ERIC search on test anxiety using EBSCO. Copyright, EBSCO Publishing, 2002. All rights reserved. Reprinted by permission.

same or a similar title (32). As with ERIC documents there is an extensive summary of this journal article (33). Descriptors (34) assigned to this article by indexers from the *Thesaurus* are provided. Examining this list of descriptors on a relevant article, we might identify other terms that could be added to our search strategy. Had we known that a particular author is an important contributor to the field we could have structured our search to find information published by that author. The disadvantage of such an author search is that many authors make contributions in more than one topic area.

A similar search might have been conducted using the print version of either *CIJE* or *RIE*. One difference is that we might have had to review many printed volumes of each index to cover the desired time. We would have had to restrict our search to the use of author, title, and subject approaches because print indexes do not provide keyword access. We would also have been unable to define our search as narrowly because in a print index we can search for only one term at a time.

An alternative to ERIC is the Education Database, which is discussed earlier in this chapter, or its printed counterpart, *EI*. If you use Education Database, the results differ from those that ERIC produces because the search engine is different, and the *EI* database covers a different set of journals from that of the ERIC database. Additionally, as noted previously, it does provide access to full text of some journals. However, the principles of searching are similar. The print version of *EI* has the same shortcomings as any printed index, that is, the inability to combine multiple terms and to use keyword searching.

BUSINESS AND MANAGEMENT

Sources Discussed

ABI/inform global. (1971–present). New York: ProQuest Information and Learning.
Business abstracts. (1982–present). New York: H. W. Wilson.
Business full text. (1995–present). New York: H. W. Wilson.
Business periodicals index. (1958–present). New York: H. W. Wilson.
Business source elite. (1984–present) Ipswich, MA: EBSCO.
LexisNexis academic universe. (1998–present). Miamisburg, OH: Reed Elsevier.

Section Example: Stress in Business Travel

In many jobs (e.g., sales/marketing and auditing) regular travel is a part of the job and a cost of doing business. In some companies expectations of career advancement may be linked, at least in part, to a willingness to travel. For executives in many organizations, frequent regular travel is required.

Whereas some people enjoy traveling on business, it is a stressful experience for others. In a telephone survey of frequent business travelers, 8 of 10 indicated that work on the road is stressful, and 5% reported that their business travel is very stressful (Fisher & Stoneman, 1998). Workers with young families experience stress when missing a child's sporting event, an anniversary, or a birthday while on the road. Many perceive that the traveling worker, spouse, and children all pay a price for the travel. Fourteen percent of frequent business travelers (more than 25 trips per year) believe business travel has hurt their marriages. A majority of frequent business travelers report some disappointment with absences from their children (Fisher & Stoneman).

Singles who travel seem to find different things stressful. They tend to have more difficulty coping with work not getting done at the office. Many also worry about unmet personal obligations, such as unpaid bills, an untended residence, accumulating mail, and untended pets (Fisher & Stoneman, 1998).

A study of staff at the World Bank reported that people who travel file more health insurance claims than nontravelers. Psychiatric insurance claims were higher for business travelers than for nontravelers, and the number of claims increased with frequency of international travel (Woods & Wilcox, 1998).

A "most stressed business traveler" contest sponsored by the Crescent Court Hotel in Dallas, Texas, yielded numerous travel horror stories. Among the tales were that of the frequent flying software support specialist who was seated next to an alcohol-consuming televangelist who alternately asked for donations and made passes, and there was the story of the consulting engineer traveling in Russia who, with other bus passengers, shoveled snow with his hands and helped push the bus back onto the local highway (Seal, 1995).

Are these reports an accurate depiction of psychological stress among business travelers? How widespread is this problem? What can business travelers do to reduce travel-related stress? We use the example of psychological stress and business travel to illustrate literature searches in the business and management literature.

Business Sources

Several primary resources existed for locating business literature as of 2002: H. W. Wilson's *Business Periodicals Index, Business Full Text,* and *Business Abstracts;* EBSCO's Business Source Elite; ABI/Inform Global; and *LexisNexis Academic Universe.*

Wilson Business Databases

The oldest of the services is H. W. Wilson Company's Business Databases. These include *Business Periodicals Index (BPI), Business Full Text,* and *Business Abstracts.* They are very similar to the *Education Index* family of products. Like the Education Databases, Business Databases are available in electronic form on CD-ROM and online through WilsonWeb. *BPI* was initiated by H. W. Wilson in 1913 as *Industrial Arts Index,* but in 1958 it was split into *BPI* and *Applied Science and Technology Index. BPI* is published monthly and cumulated annually and provided access to English-language journals on business. As of mid-2002 *Business Abstracts* provided indexing access with article abstracts to approximately 550 English-language general business periodicals and trade journals, plus *The Wall Street Journal* and business section of *The New York Times. Business Full Text* provides full-text coverage (in HTML or full-image PDF formats) of 282 periodicals beginning in 1995.

Business Source Elite

EBSCO Publishing provides Business Source Elite (BSE) in electronic form as an online bibliographic database. The BSE database includes an index and abstracts of articles from approximately 1,580 journals since 1984 in business, management, economics, and related areas. It also provides full text of articles in approximately 1,050 of these journals.

ABI/Inform Global

ProQuest Information and Learning developed ABI/Inform Global. The database contains more than 500,000 citations, with abstracts for articles in about 1,000 international periodicals in business, management, and related areas. Coverage is provided back to 1971 and includes full text of articles from some business publications starting in 1991. Like BSE, ABI/Inform Global is available only electronically.

LexisNexis

The newest of the services, the business information bibliographic database contained in LexisNexis Academic Universe, provides electronic access to business periodical literature through the World Wide Web. Its indexing and abstracting coverage of more than 400 business magazines and journals from around the world is a small portion of the resources available. Other content includes access to more than 50 English-language newspapers, news transcripts from television networks, financial information, company directories, and legal and medical information.

Each of these services is fairly expensive. As a result your library may not provide access to all of them. Become familiar with what is available to you, and learn how to use it.

Business Literature Search

Returning to our search topic, we are seeking information on psychological stress resulting from business travel. Key words for the concept of stress include *stress* and *psychological stress*. We are concerned with stress involved in *travel*. Our focus is on travel related to work rather than to play, so the following might be relevant search terms: *business, work,* and *job*.

We turn to an electronic medium to conduct our search. The first tool we use is the BSE service. We conduct an advanced search that allows us to define search parameters narrowly. The user interface screen might look something like that shown in Figure 6.7. (Note that this interface is almost the same as the one provided for the EBSCO version of ERIC.) We enter our first two search terms, travel and stress (35), as independent concepts that must both be included with a Boolean **AND** intersection (36). We are not sure, however, whether articles will address work or jobs or business, so we enter all three terms in our search, linking them as a union with a Boolean **OR** (37). We search all fields (38) rather than restrict our search. Although we could refine our search even further, specifying attributes such as a particular time period, we have not done so.

Our BSE search returned 47 references (more than 4 pages, with 10 references per page) that satisfy our search parameters. A citation is provided for each item identified. Figure 6.8 (p. 86) displays the first three items on the second page of our search. As we review the list, of particular interest is item number 12 (39). This is an article titled "Executive travel stress: Perils of the road warrior" written by Richard S. DeFrank. It appeared in May 2000 in volume 14, issue 2, of *Academy of Management Executive*. The article is 14 pages long, starts on page 58 of the printed issue, and contains two charts, one diagram, and three black-and-white pictures. We note that there is a hyperlink in the database to Full Text (40) of the article. Selecting the hyperlinked article title (39), we are able to display the full BSE citation for this journal article.

Figure 6.9 (p. 86) displays the bibliographic record for this article. It includes a brief abstract summarizing the article (41), the unique accession number (42) for this article in the database (AN: 3819306), and the ISSN (43) for the journal in which the article appeared (1079-5545). We are also provided the subject terms (44) used to index this article in the database, information that may be useful in refining or expanding our search. Had we instead selected the hyperlink for the full text (40) shown in Figure 6.8, we could have displayed on our screen an electronic copy of the article. Depending on

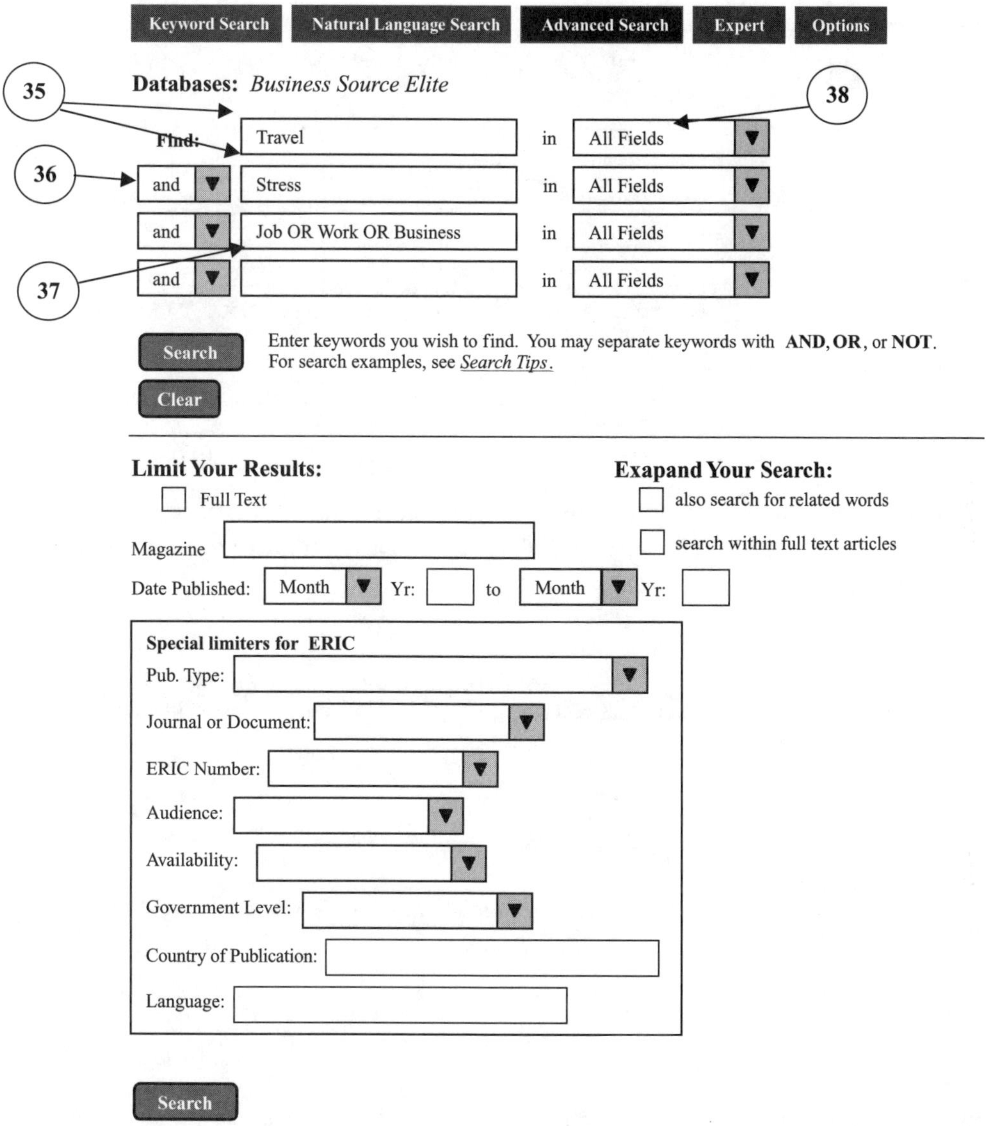

FIGURE 6.7. Sample *Business Source Elite* search on travel stress; initial screen using EBSCO. Copyright, EBSCO Publishing, 2002. All rights reserved. Reprinted by permission.

the resources of our library, we might have conducted a similar search using ABI/Inform Global, LexisNexis, or Wilson Business Database. Although results would have been different, the process of conducting the search would have been similar. If your library maintains print indexes, you might conduct your search by using volumes of *Business Periodicals Index*. Such a search has the same drawbacks as a search using *Education Index*, as discussed earlier in this chapter.

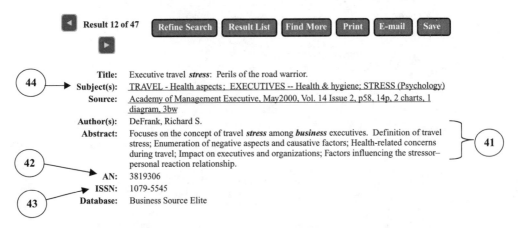

Searched: *Business Source Elite* for **TRAVEL AND (Business OR Work OR Job) AND Stress**

◄ **(11 to 20) of 47** ►   Pages: 1 2 3 4

Record	Mark	Select Result For More Detail
11.	☐	Road Warriors Feeling the Heat. Office Pro, May2000, Vol. 60 Issue 5, p5, 1/4p Full Page Image Full Text
12.	☐	Executive *travel stress*: Perils of the road warrior. By: DeFrank, Richard S.; Academy of Management Executive, May 2000, Vol. 14 Issue 2, p58, 14p, 2 charts, 1 diagram, 3bw ► Full text
13.	☐	Staying Sane in Space. By: Simpson, Sarah; Scientific American, Mar2000, Vol. 282 Issue 3, p61, 2p, 1c Full Text

(39) (40)

FIGURE 6.8. Sample Business Source Elite search results for articles on travel stress using EBSCO. Copyright, EBSCO Publishing, 2002. All rights reserved. Reprinted by permission.

◄ **Result 12 of 47**   [Refine Search] [Result List] [Find More] [Print] [E-mail] [Save]
►

Title: Executive travel *stress*: Perils of the road warrior.
Subject(s): TRAVEL - Health aspects ; EXECUTIVES -- Health & hygiene; STRESS (Psychology)
Source: Academy of Management Executive, May2000, Vol. 14 Issue 2, p58, 14p, 2 charts, 1 diagram, 3bw
Author(s): DeFrank, Richard S.
Abstract: Focuses on the concept of travel *stress* among *business* executives. Definition of travel stress; Enumeration of negative aspects and causative factors; Health-related concerns during travel; Impact on executives and organizations; Factors influencing the stressor–personal reaction relationship.
AN: 3819306
ISSN: 1079-5545
Database: Business Source Elite

(44) (42) (43) (41)

FIGURE 6.9. Sample journal article entry from a *Business Sources Elite* search on travel stress. Copyright, EBSCO Publishing, 2002. All rights reserved. Reprinted by permission.

HEALTH CARE: MEDICINE, PSYCHIATRY, NURSING, AND RELATED AREAS

Sources Discussed

CINAHL. (1951–present). Glendale, CA: CINAHL Information Systems.
Cumulated index medicus. (1960–2000). Bethesda, MD: U.S. National Library of Medicine.
Index medicus. (1960–present). Bethesda, MD: U.S. National Library of Medicine.
MEDLINE. (1960–present). Bethesda, MD: U.S. National Library of Medicine.

Section Example: Psychological Stress and Coronary Heart Disease

Stress has been identified as a risk factor in several health problems. Williams (1999) reports that an estimated 6.2 million Americans have significant coronary heart disease and estimates that an additional 12 million have undiagnosed cardiovascular disease. The link between stress and fluctuations in catecholamines and norepinephrine (adrenal hormones) suggests a stress role in coronary heart disease (Holroyd & Lazarus, 1982; Rosenman & Chesney, 1982). Summarizing prior research, Lovallo (1997) reported increased likelihood of heart attack in the 2 hours following an episode of anger and increased rates of coronary death and stroke following population threats such as earthquake.

As noted at the beginning of the chapter, an aversive (stressful) event may trigger primary threat appraisals. This emotional response may increase autonomic nervous system outflow and secretion of stress-related hormones. This can increase the demand for oxygen to the heart, aggravate stress on walls of blood vessels, and enhance clot formation. Vascular stress and clotting add to the risk of stroke (a cerebrovascular disease that affects the brain's arteries), whereas cardiac stress increases risk of myocardial infarction (heart attack, or death of heart muscle cells caused by lack of oxygen or other nutrients; Lovallo, 1997).

Sudden cardiac death may be precipitated by stress (Gomez & Gomez, 1984; Williams, 1999), and anger has been identified as a possible trigger for acute myocardial infarction (Mittleman et al., 1995). According to Lovallo (1997) stress-induced fatal heart attacks or strokes occur most often in persons who already have atherosclerosis of the coronary arteries (narrowing of the arteries because of fat buildups) or arteriosclerosis of the arteries (narrowing of the arteries because of calcium deposits) supplying the brain. Acute stress leads to activation of neuroendocrine hormones (e.g., secretion of epinephrine) as well as increase of both heart rate and blood pressure (Kozicz & Casey, 1999; Lovallo, 1997). Circulating ephinephrine can lead to clot formation (Lovallo, 1997), whereas increased heart rate and blood pressure may lead to turbulent blood flow and stress on the endothelium (a layer of smooth cells lining the blood vessels and heart), promoting internal injury (Kozicz & Casey, 1999). Yet Schneck (1997) argues for more research on the links between stress and stroke.

What more can we learn about the impact of stress on coronary heart attack and stroke as well as about prevention measures and treatment? In this section we focus on stress, heart disease, and stroke to illustrate literature searches in health and medicine.

Health Care Sources

The most comprehensive source providing access to health science literature is the series produced by the U.S. National Library of Medicine (NLM). The series, *Index Medicus,* a monthly index to the medical journal literature, began in 1960. It indexes approximately 3,000 journal titles in many languages; provides author, title, and subject access to health science literature; and was cumulated in the annual *Cumulated Index Medicus.* Intended for smaller libraries, *Abridged Index Medicus* and *Abridged Cumulated Index Medicus* indexes approximately 100 journals. Subject indexing of the literature is guided by the controlled vocabulary of Medical Subject Headings (MeSH), also developed by the NLM. The NLM ceased publication of print volumes of *Cumulated Index Medicus* with volume 41 in 2000.

The NLM is also responsible for production of MEDLINE (Medical Literature, Analysis, and Retrieval System Online). MEDLINE is an online bibliographic database of more than 11 million citations to periodical articles in the health sciences (medicine, nursing, dentistry, veterinary medicine, pharmacy, and related areas). Its worldwide coverage of more than 4,300 journals begins with 1966 and includes publications in more than 30 languages. MEDLINE indexing is guided by MeSH, which for years was used to produce the print volumes of *Index Medicus*.

The most widely available access to MEDLINE (in 2002) is through PubMed (http://www.ncbi.nlm.nih.gov/PubMed/) a worldwide Web-based retrieval service providing access to MEDLINE and developed by the National Center for Biotechnology Information (NCBI) at NLM. Like many other electronic search tools, PubMed allows searching the database in many ways, including by author, title, subject, keyword, phrase, and so on. PubMed also provides links to the electronic full text of many journal articles indexed by MEDLINE. Several bibliographic aggregators, such as EBSCO, also provide access to MEDLINE.

Health Care Literature Search

We pursue our search for information on psychological stress and coronary heart disease using the PubMed service to access MEDLINE. As with all prior searches, the definition of key terms and the structure of our search play a critical role in the information we retrieve. We structure our search as follows, defining our terms as text strings, linked with the Boolean **AND**: *psychological stress* **AND** *coronary heart disease*. This example is a phrase search in which the term *psychological* would have to appear adjacent to the term *stress* in exactly that order. In addition, this phrase has to appear in the same record as the phrase *coronary heart disease*, again with the terms in exactly that order. Note that this is a different search than the following: psychological stress **AND** coronary heart disease. In this latter search specification, although all five of these terms would have to appear in a citation to be retrieved, the order and location would be irrelevant. Our most recent PubMed searches, in December 2001, revealed radically different results: The first yielded 374 citations, the second 1272 citations. We could narrow our search further, but for the purposes of illustration here we keep it simple.

When we enter the PubMed database, we are presented with a screen such as that displayed in Figure 6.10. (PubMed also provides access to other biomedical databases, such as Nucleotides.) We could conduct a basic search, structure a more advanced search by selecting Preview/Index, or limit our search on the basis of publication type, language, age, or other factors by selecting Limits. We enter our specification for the basic search already outlined, as shown in Figure 6.10, and initiate the search of the MEDLINE database. Note that hints are provided for structuring your search. This simple search has identified 374 citations from the MEDLINE database that match the parameters of our request. The first 20 citations are returned in the initial display, in order by date of publication. Figure 6.11 displays three of the citations identified (no. 5, no. 6, and no. 7). Based on the no. 6 article's title, "Mental stress as a causal factor in the development of hypertension and cardiovascular disease," the item by T. G. Pickering appears to be relevant (45). It is identified as a review article (46). It appeared in volume 3, issue 3, of the journal *Current Hypertension Reports*, on pages 249–254 of the June 2001 issue (47). The unique PubMed identification number (PMID) (48) for this item in the database is 11353576. Selecting the hyperlinked author field for TG Pickering (49) enables display of

| PubMed | "psychological stress" AND "coronary heart disease" |

- Enter one or more search terms, or click Preview/Index for advanced searching.
- Enter author names as smith jc. Initials are optional.
- Enter journal titles in full or as MEDLINE abbreviations. Use the Journal Browser to find journal titles.

> PubMed, a service of the National Library of Medicine, provides access to over 11 million MEDLINE citations back to the mid-1960's and additional life science journals. PubMed includes links to many sites providing full text articles and other related resources

FIGURE 6.10. Example of an initial user interface screen for PubMed for a MEDLINE search.

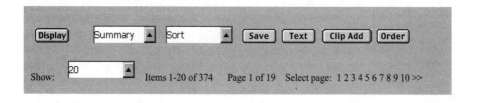

Display   Summary ▲   Sort ▲   Save   Text   Clip Add   Order

Show: 20 ▲   Items 1-20 of 374   Page 1 of 19   Select page: 1 2 3 4 5 6 7 8 9 10 >>

• • •

5: Sarabi M, Lind L.
Mental stress opposes endothelium-dependent vasodilation in young healthy individuals.
Vasc Med. 2001;6(1):3–7.
49 PMID: 11358157 [PubMed—indexed for MEDLINE]

45 6: Pickering TG.
Mental stress as a causal factor in the development of hypertension and
47 cardiovascular disease.
Curr Hypertens Rep. 2001 Jun;3(3):249–54. Review.
PMID: 11353576 [PubMed—indexed for MEDLINE] **46**
48

7: Zhang J, Vitaliano PP, Lutgendorf SK, Scanlan JM, Savage MV.
Sense of coherence buffers relationships of chronic stress with fasting glucose levels.
J Behav Med. 2001 Feb;24(1):33–55.
PMID: 11296469 [PubMed—indexed for MEDLINE].

• • •

FIGURE 6.11. Example of partial results from a MEDLINE search using PubMed.

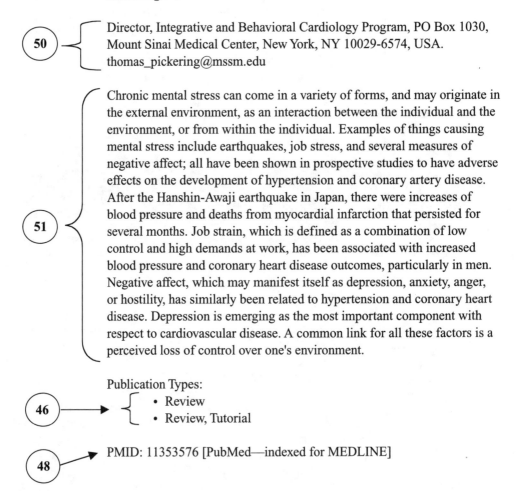

Curr Hypertens Rep 2001 Jun;3(3):249–54

CURRENT *reports*

Mental stress as a causal factor in the development of hypertension and cardiovascular disease.

Pickering TG.

(50) Director, Integrative and Behavioral Cardiology Program, PO Box 1030, Mount Sinai Medical Center, New York, NY 10029-6574, USA. thomas_pickering@mssm.edu

(51) Chronic mental stress can come in a variety of forms, and may originate in the external environment, as an interaction between the individual and the environment, or from within the individual. Examples of things causing mental stress include earthquakes, job stress, and several measures of negative affect; all have been shown in prospective studies to have adverse effects on the development of hypertension and coronary artery disease. After the Hanshin-Awaji earthquake in Japan, there were increases of blood pressure and deaths from myocardial infarction that persisted for several months. Job strain, which is defined as a combination of low control and high demands at work, has been associated with increased blood pressure and coronary heart disease outcomes, particularly in men. Negative affect, which may manifest itself as depression, anxiety, anger, or hostility, has similarly been related to hypertension and coronary heart disease. Depression is emerging as the most important component with respect to cardiovascular disease. A common link for all these factors is a perceived loss of control over one's environment.

Publication Types:
(46)   • Review
        • Review, Tutorial

(48)   PMID: 11353576 [PubMed—indexed for MEDLINE]

FIGURE 6.12. Example of a MEDLINE PubMed bibliographic entry.

the full MEDLINE entry for this item. Figure 6.12 displays the full MEDLINE entry for the Pickering citation. In addition to the usual citation information (source, title, author), this record contains institutional affiliation, address and e-mail address information for the author (50), and an abstract of the article (51). The note that this is a review (46) and the PMID number is included (48).

An alternative source that some may find useful is CINAHL (Cumulative Index to Nursing and Allied Health Literature). As the title suggests, its focus is on literature in nursing. Its focus is narrower than that of MEDLINE, covering only about 950 journals, and much of what is indexed in CINAHL is also in MEDLINE. The advantage of CINAHL is that it does have some full-text entries, including the ProQuest Nursing Journals.

SOCIOLOGY

Sources Discussed

Social work abstracts. (1977-present). Washington, DC: National Association of Social Workers. Previous titles: *Social Work Research and Abstracts*.
Sociological abstracts. (1962–present). San Diego, CA: Sociological Abstracts.
Sociological abstracts, LLC. (1999). *Thesaurus of sociological indexing terms* (5th ed.). Bethesda, MD: Cambridge Scientific Abstracts.

Section Example: Psychological Stress and Urban Environment

To what extent does urbanization induce psychological stress, which results in other problems for individuals? Humans have need for community (a feeling of belongingness). Whereas some people feel a sense of community in the city, others may find the city alienating (Henslin, 1993). Herbert Gans (1962), in his book *The Urban Villagers*, reported on the existence of communities with extensive networks of friendships in spite of environmental problems (e.g., substandard buildings, garbage). He also reported on those who were deprived or trapped in their environment: poor people, persons with disabilities, people who are downwardly mobile, and older people, as well as persons with substance abuse problems.

Mark Baldassare (1979) noted that research on animals suggests that crowding leads to stress, which leads to pathological problems. However, there are differences between species; animal models may be too simplistic. Psychological stress involves a perception of frustration, overload, or other imbalance, and because people attempt to exercise control over their environments, the extent to which urbanization leads to the perception of stress is complex. Thus we cannot conclude that because people live in an urban environment they are stressed and suffer severe psychological problems. Groups with less social power might face psychological problems to a greater extent as they have less ability to control their environments (Baldassare, 1979).

David Glass characterized city life as "an endless round of obstacles, conflicts, inconveniences, and bureaucratic routine . . . with noise, litter, air pollution, and overcrowding . . . capable of producing a stress response" (Glass, 1972, pp. 5–6). He noted that we may attempt to reduce stress through adaptation and habituation. Continued exposure to stress may produce cumulative long-term effects, and the constant act of vigilant coping may itself be stressful. His research on noise indicated that noise impairs performance. He concluded that uncontrollable noise sources in our urban environment make it "almost unbearable and, indeed, dangerous for behavioral efficiency and mental well-being" (Glass, 1972, p. 162). Henslin (1993) suggested that city dwellers take steps to protect themselves: They use filters to reduce overload, avoid encounters with strangers, and protect personal space.

More recently, in reviewing research on the impact of unhealthy environments, Taylor, Repetti, and Seeman (1997) noted that relationships between environmental factors and genetic predispositions result in significant variability in individual susceptibility to psychological stress and mental or physical health consequences of stress. They suggest that persons who are better able to cope with their unhealthy environments may be less susceptible to stress. Socioeconomic status (SES) may be a mediator of stress such that the lower the SES, the more people are subjected to stress: They must spend more time addressing the basic tasks of living, they are affected by crime, they are denied more services, they have poorer transportation, and so forth (Taylor, Repetti, & Seeman, 1997).

What more can we learn about urbanization (crowding, noise, pollution, etc.) as a cause of stress? What are the consequences of stress on the family, urban institutions, and mental health of city dwellers? In this section we focus on stress and its consequences for urbanization to illustrate literature searches in sociology and social work.

Sociology Sources

Sociological Abstracts (*SA*) is the primary index to the research literature of sociology, including many interdisciplinary areas such as community development, demography, evaluation research, group interaction, social development, and women's studies. *SA* provides coverage back to 1953 and added abstracts of articles in 1974. At present it covers approximately 2,600 journals and serials as well as conference papers, books, and dissertations. An electronic version of the Sociological Abstracts Database is available from Cambridge Scientific Abstracts, OCLC FirstSearch, and other vendors.

You might also consult *Social Work Abstracts (SWA)*. This is the primary index providing access to literature on social work and social welfare. Initiated in 1977, *SWA* is available electronically on the Web, in CD-ROM form, and in hard copy.

Sociology Search

Our search focuses on the consequences of stress on the family, urban institutions, and mental health of city dwellers. Recognizing that articles may refer to the geographic location of interest as either city or urban, we can structure our search using the following keywords: *psychological stress* **AND** (*city* **OR** *urban*) **AND** *family*. At this point we keep our search simple. Our access to *SA* is through the online interface provided by Cambridge Scientific Abstracts, demonstrated in chapter 5. Our search returns 15 citations. When we request only citations, search results looked like the two citation examples in Figure 6.13. Here we have only the citation for the articles (51), including information on title (TI), author (AU), and source (SO). Note also that at the top of the page, the database in use (52) and the search requested (53) are both provided.

Suppose we had requested the fully expanded entry for item 8 of the 15 returned by our search. This is illustrated in Figure 6.14 (p. 94). It appears to have a great deal of similarity to the format and contents of a PsycINFO bibliographic record (discussed in chapter 5). Standard bibliographic information is provided about this

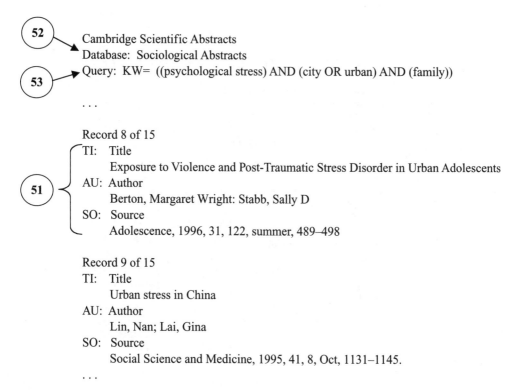

52

Cambridge Scientific Abstracts
Database: Sociological Abstracts

53

Query: KW= ((psychological stress) AND (city OR urban) AND (family))

. . .

Record 8 of 15

51

TI: Title
        Exposure to Violence and Post-Traumatic Stress Disorder in Urban Adolescents
AU: Author
        Berton, Margaret Wright: Stabb, Sally D
SO: Source
        Adolescence, 1996, 31, 122, summer, 489–498

Record 9 of 15
TI: Title
        Urban stress in China
AU: Author
        Lin, Nan; Lai, Gina
SO: Source
        Social Science and Medicine, 1995, 41, 8, Oct, 1131–1145.

. . .

FIGURE 6.13. Example of brief form of results from *Sociological Abstracts* search. Published by Cambridge Scientific Abstracts. Reprinted by permission.

article (54): title, authors, source, and the ISSN. An abstract summarizes the article, and we learn that the article is written in English (55). The record provides descriptors used to index the article and identifiers attached to the article as well as the general classification into which the article is grouped (56). This is unique item number 9615942 in the *SA* database (57).

As with other searches, we continue reviewing other items identified in our search for their applicability to our topic. We may also wish to redefine and rerun our search to ensure that we have identified all relevant sources. For a different perspective we could also consult *Social Work Abstracts*. Just as clinical and experimental psychologists approach the world from different perspectives, so do sociologists and social workers. Thus the coverage of issues related to public policy and mental health implications of urban stress in the literature of sociology would differ from that in social work.

Throughout this chapter we have attempted to encourage you to be aware of the larger context in which many psychologists work. Whereas some psychologists engage in research that occupies a very narrow scope, people in other disciplines address broad areas of psychological inquiry. When engaging in research in such areas, it is important to be aware of these different points of view. To do this may require using some of the tools of the other disciplines that we have discussed in this chapter.

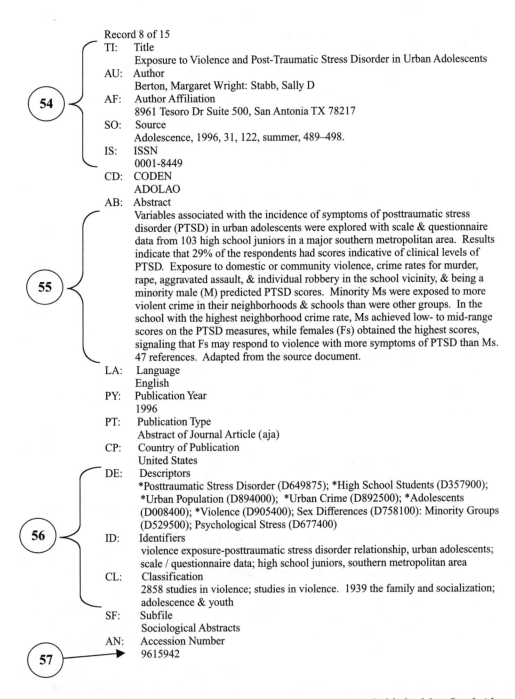

Record 8 of 15
TI: Title
       Exposure to Violence and Post-Traumatic Stress Disorder in Urban Adolescents
AU: Author
       Berton, Margaret Wright: Stabb, Sally D
AF: Author Affiliation
       8961 Tesoro Dr Suite 500, San Antonia TX 78217
SO: Source
       Adolescence, 1996, 31, 122, summer, 489–498.
IS: ISSN
       0001-8449
CD: CODEN
       ADOLAO
AB: Abstract
       Variables associated with the incidence of symptoms of posttraumatic stress
       disorder (PTSD) in urban adolescents were explored with scale & questionnaire
       data with 103 high school juniors in a major southern metropolitan area. Results
       indicate that 29% of the respondents had scores indicative of clinical levels of
       PTSD. Exposure to domestic or community violence, crime rates for murder,
       rape, aggravated assault, & individual robbery in the school vicinity, & being a
       minority male (M) predicted PTSD scores. Minority Ms were exposed to more
       violent crime in their neighborhoods & schools than were other groups. In the
       school with the highest neighborhood crime rate, Ms achieved low- to mid-range
       scores on the PTSD measures, while females (Fs) obtained the highest scores,
       signaling that Fs may respond to violence with more symptoms of PTSD than Ms.
       47 references. Adapted from the source document.
LA: Language
       English
PY: Publication Year
       1996
PT: Publication Type
       Abstract of Journal Article (aja)
CP: Country of Publication
       United States
DE: Descriptors
       *Posttraumatic Stress Disorder (D649875); *High School Students (D357900);
       *Urban Population (D894000); *Urban Crime (D892500); *Adolescents
       (D008400); *Violence (D905400); Sex Differences (D758100): Minority Groups
       (D529500); Psychological Stress (D677400)
ID: Identifiers
       violence exposure-posttraumatic stress disorder relationship, urban adolescents;
       scale / questionnaire data; high school juniors, southern metropolitan area
CL: Classification
       2858 studies in violence; studies in violence. 1939 the family and socialization;
       adolescence & youth
SF: Subfile
       Sociological Abstracts
AN: Accession Number
       9615942

FIGURE 6.14. Example of a full entry from *Sociological Abstracts*. Published by Cambridge Scientific Abstracts. Reprinted by permission.

REFERENCES

Baldassare, M. (1979). *Residential crowding in urban America*. Berkeley, CA: University of California Press.

Beidel, D. C., Turner, S. M., & Taylor-Ferreira, J. C. (1999). Teaching study skills and test-taking strategies to elementary school students: The Testburner program. *Behavior Modification, 23*, 630–646.

Cannon, W. B. (1932). *The wisdom of the body*. New York: Norton.

Fisher, C., & Stoneman, B. (1998, June). Business on the road. *American Demographics, 20*(6), 44–47.

Gans, H. J. (1962). *The urban villagers*. New York: Free Press.

Glass, D. C. (1972). *Urban stress: Experiments on noise and social stressors*. New York: Academic Press.

Goldberger, L., & Breznitz, S. (Eds.). (1982). *Handbook of stress: Theoretical and clinical aspects*. New York: Free Press.

Gomez, G. E., & Gomez, E. A. (1984). Sudden death, biopsychosocial factors. *Heart & Lung, 13*, 389.

Henslin, J. M. (1993). *Sociology: A down-to-earth approach*. Boston: Allyn & Bacon.

Holroyd, J. A., & Lazarus, R. S. (1982). Stress, coping, and somatic adaptation. In L. Goldberger & S. Breznitz (Eds.), *Handbook of stress: Theoretical and clinical aspects* (pp. 21–35). New York: Free Press.

Kozicz, S. L., & Casey, A. (1999). Stress management. In N. Jairath (Ed.), *Coronary heart disease and risk factor management: A nursing perspective* (pp. 204–218). Philadelphia: W. B. Saunders.

Lazarus, R., & Folkman, S. (1984). *Stress, appraisal, and coping*. New York: Springer.

Lazarus, R. S. (1966). *Psychological stress and the coping process*. New York: McGraw-Hill.

Lovallo, W. R. (1997). *Stress and health: Biological and psychological interactions*. Thousand Oaks, CA: Sage .

McDonald, A. S. (2001). The prevalence and effects of test anxiety in school children. *Educational Psychology, 21*, 89–101.

Mittleman, M., Maclure, M., Sherwood, J., Mulry, R., Tofler, G., Jacobs, S., et al. (1995). Triggering of acute myocardial infarction onset by episodes of anger. *Circulation, 92*, 1720–1725.

Rosenman, R. H., & Chesney, M.A. (1982). Stress, Type A behavior, and coronary disease. In L. Goldberger & S. Breznitz (Eds.), *Handbook of stress: Theoretical and clinical aspects* (pp. 547–565). New York: Free Press.

Sarason, I. G. (1980). Introduction to the study of test anxiety. In I. G. Sarason (Ed.), *Test anxiety: Theory, research, and applications* (pp. 3–14). Hillsdale, NJ: Erlbaum.

Sarason, I. G. (1984). Stress, anxiety, and cognitive interference: Reaction to tests. *Journal of Personality and Social Psychology, 46*, 929–938.

Schneck, M. J. (1997). Is psychological stress a risk factor for cerebral disease? *Neuroepidemiology, 16*, 174–179.

Seal, K. (1995, Jan. 9). Survey uncovers wacky tales of business-travel stress. *Hotel & Motel Management, 210*(1), 8–9.

Selye, H. (1956). *The stress of life*. New York: McGraw-Hill.

Sieber, J. E. (1980). Defining test anxiety: Problems and approaches. In I. G. Sarason (Ed.), *Test anxiety: Theory, research, and applications* (pp. 15–40). Hillsdale, NJ: Erlbaum.

Steptoe, A., & Appels, A. (1989). *Stress, personal control, and health*. New York: John Wiley.

Sternberg, R. J. (1996). *Successful intelligence: How practical and creative intelligence determine success in life*. New York: Simon & Schuster.

Taylor, S. E., Repetti, R. L., & Seeman, T. (1997). Health psychology: What is an unhealthy environment and how does it get under the skin? In J. T Spence, J. M. Darley, & D. J. Foss (Eds.), *Annual review of psychology* (Vol. 48, pp. 411–447). Palo Alto, CA: Annual Reviews.

Williams, D. (1999). Nursing assessment. In N. Jairath (Ed.), *Coronary heart disease & risk factor management: A nursing perspective*. Philadelphia: W. B. Saunders.

Woods, L., & Wilcox, M. D. (1998, March). Business travelers battle the blues. *Kiplinger's Personal Finance Magazine, 52*(3), 24.

7 Citation Searching

Sources Discussed

Social sciences citation index (SSCI). (1956–present). Philadelphia: Institute for Scientific Information.

WHY CITATION SEARCHING?

RESEARCH IN a field changes as authors offer new empirical data, new theories, or new interpretations of existing theories, or as they review a body of work. Reports may point researchers in new directions and in some cases initiate new areas of investigation. Searching by subject depends on one's knowledge of the terminology in a field. Searching by subject or using a subject index may yield relevant information. A subject search, however, may not identify relevant information if the searcher has not used the correct terminology. It also does not necessarily trace the linkages in a field, that is, indicate who has been influenced by whom.

The concept of using cited references in articles is discussed briefly in chapter 5. The strength of PsycINFO and most other databases is their extensive subject access to research literature. Citation searching provides an alternative to subject searching and a mechanism for identifying influences in a field. To search using citations, you do not need to rely on subject headings, indexing terms, or the specific vocabulary used by authors. Citation indexes are based on the premise that published research includes references to previously published reports that provide the theoretical and empirical context for the new paper. In turn, this premise is based on the assumption that researchers have located and reported previously published citations that serve as a basis and inspiration for their own research. If you can identify an important early source in an area, you should be able to identify subsequent articles that refer to the earlier source.

CHAPTER EXAMPLE: SEMANTIC INFORMATION RETRIEVAL FROM MEMORY

Thousands of years ago, even a few hundred years ago, most people did not read. In some cultures there was no written language; verbal communication was the norm for most of the population. In today's world, however, reading is a skill required for effective functioning in society and in most jobs. Reading is a complex, learned task. It involves perception, intelligence, memory, thinking, and knowledge of the language. Why is reading so difficult? According to Sternberg (1999), the process seems to work something like this: We perceive visual symbols (e.g., letters) that we translate into sounds, we assemble these sounds into a word, and we search our memories to find and recall the meaning of the word. We move on to the next word, combining the individual word meanings into a message, and repeat the process until we reach the end of the sentence. Sternberg suggested that there are two basic types of processes at work: lexical processes (identifying letters and words and activating relevant information in memory) and comprehension processes (making sense of the text we read). It is the lexical process that allows us to gain access to the meaning of a word from memory.

In studying memory several years ago, Meyer and Schvaneveldt (1976) reported some interesting findings on the retrieval of verbal information from memory (a lexical process). They conducted a series of sentence comprehension experiments to study retrieval of semantic information about words. In one experiment subjects were asked to verify the truth or falsehood of a series of affirmative sentences. Speed of retrieval of information differed based on relatedness of concepts contained in the sentences; reaction times were shorter when meanings of categories of words were more closely related (e.g., "some pines are trees" vs. "some writers are mothers"). In another experiment subjects read a series of letters and had to decide whether letters formed a word (e.g., nurse, butter) or not (e.g., nart, trief). Meyer and Schvaneveldt found that subjects recognized a word more quickly if it followed another related word (e.g., bread, butter) than if it followed an unrelated word. Arguing that context is important, they suggested that human memory "includes a semantic network that represents various categories of objects at distinct locations linked to specify their relations with each other" (p. 32).

Suppose we wish to pursue the work of Meyer and Schvaneveldt (1976) on stored semantic information retrieval to determine whether it has been replicated, supported, or refuted. How might we do this? One method is to conduct a citation search, to identify those authors who have reported research in which they cited this study. In this chapter we discuss the principles of citation searching by using Meyer and Schvaneveldt as the source.

SOCIAL SCIENCES CITATION INDEX

Initiated in 1969, *Social Sciences Citation Index (SSCI)* provides complete coverage of about 1,700 journals and selective coverage of an additional 3,300 journals in the social sciences. Among the disciplines it covers are anthropology, business, communication, psychology, and sociology. *SSCI* indexes articles, books, editorials, book reviews, conference reports, and conference proceedings. *SSCI* is distributed in a variety of formats (print, CD-ROM, Web-based). Frequency of updates varies with the format, for example, weekly on the Web versus monthly on CD-ROM. Index coverage dates back to 1956, and abstracts for most articles date back to 1992. Companion series include *Science Citation Index*, initiated in 1963 (with coverage back to 1945), and *Arts and Humanities Citation Index*, begun in 1978 (with coverage back to 1975). In 1997, the Institute for Scientific Information (ISI) launched its Web of Science, which provides access to all three citation index products. Since 2001 Web of Science has been incorporated into ISI's more comprehensive Web of Knowledge.

Because of their cost, citation indexes have traditionally been restricted to large libraries serving graduate students and researchers. Fortunately, differential pricing for large and small campuses means that more small libraries can afford *SSCI* access. As with other electronic database products, the *SSCI* user interface screens change from time to time. In addition, other database products are developing features that take advantage of citation searching.

CITATION SEARCH EXAMPLE

Conceptually, the citation search is an iterative one, built sequentially by checking references of references of references. As illustrated in Figure 7.1, assume that article A is a highly relevant early source. Then suppose that articles B, C, D, and E all cite it. A citation search identifies these linkages. On review, we might find that B and E are important sources that add new learning to the field, whereas C and D are peripheral and therefore not an important part of research literature. We would then perform citation searches and learn that sources F, G, H, I, J, and K refer to citations B and E. We might determine that G and I are especially important and then conduct a subsequent round of searches. By doing this we identify the literature that is relevant to our topic and that represents significant contributions to our understanding, either through empirical contributions or reviews and analyses of the literature.

In conducting our sample search, we limit our efforts to the electronic version of *SSCI* in the Web of Science. Electronic versions provide a variety of search approaches,

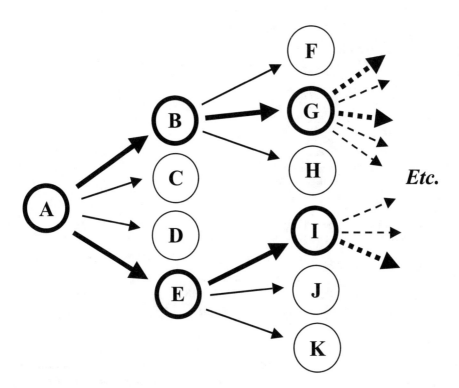

FIGURE 7.1. Logical schema of the citation search.

including that of primary author of an article. Our focus is on searching by citation, a method known to *SSCI* as the cited reference search.

Searching *SSCI* begins with an accurate citation. In this case our citation is the article "Meaning, Memory Structure, and Mental Processes" by David E. Meyer and Roger W. Schvaneveldt, published in *Science,* volume 192, issue 4234, in April 1976, on pages 27–33. We gain access to the Web of Science search engine and select the *SSCI* database. We select the option to search by cited author/reference. Through a subsequent set of user interface screens we provide the *SSCI* search engine the following information on our citation:

> Author = Meyer DE
>
> Year = 1976
>
> Cited work = Science
>
> Volume = 192
>
> Page = 27

Our search request identified 32 sources that cited this article. Figure 7.2 illustrates three items contained in the first page of the summary search results: item 8 by Larkin, Woltz, and Reynolds; item 9 by MacLeod; and item 10 by Yaniv, Meyer, and Davidson (1995). The search includes a citation for each item identified.

Cited Reference Search Results—Summary

Cited Author=Meyer D*; Cited Work=science; Cited Year=1976; DocType=All document types; Language=All languages; Databases=SSCI; Timespan=All Years; (sorted by latest date)

Page 1 (Articles 1–10):

. . .

8   Larkin AA, Woltz DJ, Reynolds RE et al.
     <u>Conceptual priming differences and reading ability</u>
     CONTEMP EDUC PSYCHOL 21 (3):279–303 JUL 1996

9   MacLeod CM
     <u>How priming affects two speeded implicit tests of remembering: Naming colors versus reading words</u>
     CONSCIOUS COGN 5 (1–2): 73–90 MAR–JUN 1996

10   YANIV I, MEYER DE, DAVIDSON NS
     <u>DYNAMIC MEMORY PROCESSES IN RETRIEVING ANSWERS TO QUESTIONS—RECALL FAILURES, JUDGMENTS Of KNOWING, AND ACQUISITION Of INFORMATION</u>
     J EXP PSYCHOL LEARN 21 (6): 1509–1521 NOV 1995

. . .

FIGURE 7.2.   Summary of a sample citation search using *SSCI*. Reprinted by permission from ISI Web of Science, Social Sciences Citation Index. © Institute for Scientific Information, Philadelphia, PA.

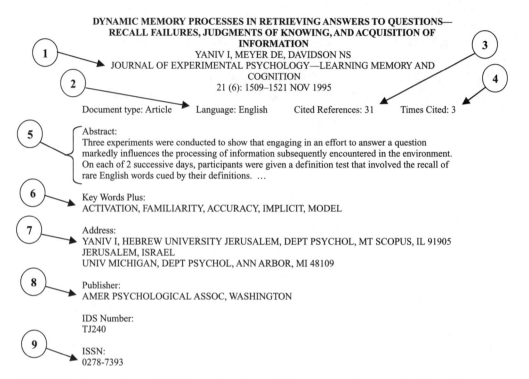

Search Results–Full Record

Article 10 of 32

DYNAMIC MEMORY PROCESSES IN RETRIEVING ANSWERS TO QUESTIONS—
RECALL FAILURES, JUDGMENTS OF KNOWING, AND ACQUISITION OF
INFORMATION
YANIV I, MEYER DE, DAVIDSON NS
JOURNAL OF EXPERIMENTAL PSYCHOLOGY—LEARNING MEMORY AND
COGNITION
21 (6): 1509–1521 NOV 1995

Document type: Article   Language: English   Cited References: 31   Times Cited: 3

Abstract:
Three experiments were conducted to show that engaging in an effort to answer a question
markedly influences the processing of information subsequently encountered in the environment.
On each of 2 successive days, participants were given a definition test that involved the recall of
rare English words cued by their definitions. ...

Key Words Plus:
ACTIVATION, FAMILIARITY, ACCURACY, IMPLICIT, MODEL

Address:
YANIV I, HEBREW UNIVERSITY JERUSALEM, DEPT PSYCHOL, MT SCOPUS, IL 91905
JERUSALEM, ISRAEL
UNIV MICHIGAN, DEPT PSYCHOL, ANN ARBOR, MI 48109

Publisher:
AMER PSYCHOLOGICAL ASSOC, WASHINGTON

IDS Number:
TJ240

ISSN:
0278-7393

FIGURE 7.3. Example of a Full Record for Item 10 from a citation search using *SSCI*.
Reprinted by permission from ISI Web of Science, Social Sciences Citation Index.
© Institute for Scientific Information, Philadelphia, PA.

If we select the hyperlinked (underlined) title of an article, we are able to learn more about the reference, as illustrated in Figure 7.3 for the Yaniv et al. (1995) article. Here we find the full title of the journal (1), not provided in the summary in Figure 7.2. This article was published in English (2), contained 31 references (3), and was cited three times by other authors (4). An abstract (5) of the article is provided along with the keywords (6) used to identify the subject content of the articles for the print indexes and for an electronic subject search. The address of the first author (7) is identified, along with the publisher (8) of the journal and the International Standard Serial Number (ISSN; 9).

If we decide that the Yaniv et al. (1995) article is relevant for our purposes, we can expand our resources by conducting a subsequent citation search looking for the three articles that cited it. Additionally, we can conduct other citation searches to expand our body of resources.

Citation searching can be a valuable supplement to the subject and keyword methods afforded by other indexes because it does not rely on a standardized subject heading approach or knowledge of the vocabulary associated with concepts. However, *SSCI* is compiled directly from reference lists as they appear in journals and therefore depends on the authors' accuracy when they compile their lists. An inaccurately cited article renders that article irretrievable in a citation-based search.

REFERENCES

Meyer, D. E., & Schvaneveldt, R. W. (1976, April 2). Meaning, memory structure, and mental processes. *Science, 192* (4234), 27–33.

Sternberg, R. J. (1999). *Cognitive psychology* (2nd ed.). Fort Worth, TX: Harcourt.

Yaniv, I., Meyer, D. E., & Davidson, N. S. (1995). Dynamic memory processes in retrieving answers to questions—recall failures, judgments of knowing, and acquisition of information. *Journal of Experimental Psychology: Learning, Memory, and Cognition, 21,* 1509–1521.

8 Government Publications

Sources Discussed

Library of Congress. Exchange and Gifts Division. (1910–1994). *Monthly checklist of state publications*. Washington, DC: U.S. Government Printing Office.

United Nations Dag Hammarskjöld Library. (1979–present). United Nations bibliographic information system. New York: United Nations. Available from http://www.un.org /Depts/dhl/dls.htm

University of Illinois at Urbana-Champaign, Documents Library. (1996–present). StateList: The electronic source for state publication lists. Retrieved March 11, 2002, from http://www.library.uiuc.edu/doc/StateList/check/check.htm

U.S. National Technical Information Service. (1990–present). NTIS product search. Washington, DC: NTIS. Available from http://www.ntis.gov/products/

U.S. Superintendent of Documents. (1994–present). *Catalog of United States government publications*. Washington, DC: U.S. Government Printing Office. Available from http://www.access.gpo.gov/su_docs/locators/cgp/index.html

U.S. Superintendent of Documents. (1994–present). GPO access. Washington, DC: U.S. Government Printing Office. Available from http://www.access.gpo.gov/su_docs /index.html

U.S. Superintendent of Documents. (1895–present). *Monthly catalog of United States government publications*. Washington, DC: U.S. Government Printing Office.

WHAT ARE GOVERNMENT PUBLICATIONS?

GOVERNMENT PUBLICATIONS are materials published and issued by federal, regional, state, local, foreign, and international governmental organizations. Issuing agencies may be part of an executive, legislative, or judicial body, or they may be independent regulatory agencies. Publications are produced in every size possible, from a single page to a multivolume set. They are available on just about any topic.

In this chapter we focus attention on publications of the U.S. federal government. These publications are distributed widely and are available throughout the United States. The federal government, through the U.S. Government Printing Office (GPO), is the largest single publisher in the United States. Publications issued include census information, federal regulations, Internal Revenue Service tax forms, congressional documents, and laws. In 2000 the GPO distributed more than 46 million printed publications, and approximately 9,000 titles are available for purchase at any time (U.S. Government

Printing Office, 2002). Increasing quantities of federal publications are issued in electronic form, and some are available on the Internet or on other electronic media.

State, international, and other government publications are also available. For example, the United Nations and its subsidiary agencies issue many documents each year. They tend to be less widely distributed and less accessible. Therefore, we mention them only briefly.

We chose to discuss government publications in a separate chapter for several reasons. Many publications issued by government bodies are not covered by the various indexing and abstracting services discussed earlier in this book. A variety of abstracts and indexes provide access to government publications. Also, many libraries with a sizable collection of government publications handle these materials separately from other materials.

The Federal Depository Libraries Program was established in 1813 to make government information widely available for free public use. More than 1,300 college, university, public, government, and special libraries in the United States have been designated federal depository libraries. On a daily basis, these libraries receive free shipments of federal publications in series they request. In 2000 the GPO distributed 12.2 million copies of more than 29,000 document titles to depository libraries (U.S. Government Printing Office, 1999). GPO Access, a resource discussed later in this chapter, allows you to locate depository libraries in specific geographic areas. You may purchase publications from the GPO by mail, online, or from one of 19 GPO bookstores throughout the country.

CHAPTER EXAMPLE: ALZHEIMER'S DISEASE

In this chapter we focus on Alzheimer's disease to illustrate the search for government publications. What is Alzheimer's disease? How do people with Alzheimer's disease change? What is their prognosis?

Alzheimer's disease is a progressive, neurodegenerative brain disorder. It is the most common cause of dementia (a condition that disrupts brain function) in older people. It is characterized by memory loss, language deterioration, poor judgment, and impaired visual and spatial skills. Confusion and restlessness may also occur. The disease usually begins after age 65 but may begin as early as age 40. It starts slowly, with early symptoms being only mild forgetfulness. As the disease progresses symptoms become easily recognizable, and eventually an individual may have difficulty with even the simplest tasks, such as brushing teeth or combing hair. An estimated 4 million people in the United States suffer from the disease. During the past few decades understanding of the disease has grown. Today it is recognized as a significant public health problem, with a major impact on millions of American families (McNeil, 1995; U.S. National Institute on Aging, 1995; U.S. National Institute of Neurological Disorders and Stroke, 2000), and with a significant economic impact (Souêtré, Thwaites, & Yeardley, 1999).

There is no known cure for Alzheimer's disease, the cause is not understood, and no confirmed method exists to slow the progress of the disease (van Reekum, Simard, & Cohen, 1999). Research is ongoing to improve understanding of the causes and prevention of the disease. Scientists are attempting to develop a test to predict its occurrence. Other research is focused on helping patients and caregivers cope with it (McNeil, 1995; U.S. National Institute on Aging, 1995; U.S. National Institute of Neurological Disorders and Stroke, 2000).

Because of the public policy implications of Alzheimer's disease, the government is an abundant source of information on this topic. It makes available information related to basic research, treatment, housing, and family support. The government is also a source of data on the disease and social policy.

This chapter focuses on the mechanisms for locating government publications. This search supplements a search for monographs and periodical articles using resources described elsewhere in this book. The most important questions are the following: How are government publications organized? How can the relevant ones be located?

ACCESS TO U.S. FEDERAL GOVERNMENT PUBLICATIONS

Many nondepository libraries order, receive, catalog, and arrange government publications in the same way they handle materials from commercial publishers. They may catalog and shelve government monographs with other books and government periodicals with other periodicals. Depository libraries, however, receive so many federal publications that they tend to handle them separately from other library materials.

Most depository libraries organize documents according to the Superintendent of Documents (SuDoc) Classification number system. The SuDoc system, developed approximately 100 years ago, has expanded and changed as the federal government has changed.

The SuDoc system is a fairly complex alphanumeric notation system. Let us examine the SuDoc number for a sample publication, *Aging in the Eighties* (SuDoc number HE 20.6209/3:124). Table 8.1 provides information about this number. The letters at the beginning identify the parent department; HE indicates that this document is issued by an agency within the Department of Health and Human Services (HHS). (The HE code is an artifact from the days when the agency was known as the Department of Health, Education and Welfare.) Departments are subdivided into bureaus, offices, and agencies, all indicated alphanumerically. The Public Health Service (HE 20) is a major agency within HHS, and the National Center for Health Statistics is an agency within the Public Health Service. Publications issued by the National Center for Health Statistics fall within the code range of HE 20.6201 to HE 20.6519. *Aging in the Eighties* is a part of the series "Advance Data From Vital & Health Statistics" (code 6209/3). A colon precedes the number, which identifies this publication as document 124. The SuDoc system was designed

TABLE 8.1. Analysis of a Sample Superintendent of Documents (SuDoc) classification System Number (HE 20.6209/3:124)

Component	SuDoc Number	
Agency	HE	Department of Health & Human Services
Subagency	20	Public Health Service
	6201–6519	National Center for Vital and Health Statistics
Series	6209/3	Advance data from Vital & Health Statistics
Publication	124	*Aging in the Eighties, Age 65 Years and Over-Use of Community Services*

TABLE 8.2. Examples of Issuing Agency Prefix Codes

Stage	Topic Statement
CR	Civil Rights Commission
ED	Department of Education
GA	General Accounting Office
HE	Department of Health and Human Services
HE 20	Public Health Service
HE 20. 3000	National Institutes of Health
HE 20. 8100	National Institute of Mental Health
HH	Department of Housing and Urban Development
L	Department of Labor
NS	National Science Foundation
L 35	Occupational Safety and Health Administration
Y 3.EQ	Equal Employment Opportunity Commission

to group publications by government agency. As can be seen in Table 8.2, there are several agencies of potential interest to psychologists. For example, publications by offices or bureaus within the Department of Education are organized with other department publications under the prefix ED. National Institute of Mental Health (NIMH) publications are organized under HE 20.8100. However, agencies in addition to the Department of Education publish documents relating to education, just as agencies other than NIMH issue publications relating to mental health. For this reason, publications on the same general topic are scattered throughout the collection of federal documents. In addition, the structure of the federal government has changed throughout the years. Educational materials were once issued by the Education Bureau in the Interior Department (code I 16), which transferred to the Federal Security Agency (code FS), which became the Department of Health, Education and Welfare, later known as the Department of Health and Human Services (code HE). In 1979 a separate cabinet-level Department of Education was created (code ED). Thus you must rely on indexes to negotiate the mass of federal publications.

The primary index to federal government publications is the *Catalog of United States Government Publications*, produced by the U.S. Superintendent of Documents. It indexes print and electronic documents produced and issued by federal government agencies. Initiated in January 1994, it is available electronically on the Internet through GPO Access, a Web site maintained by the GPO. The print equivalent of the *Catalog* is the *Monthly Catalog of United States Government Publications (MoCat)*, which has been published since 1895. If you are looking for government documents issued before 1994, you must consult *MoCat*. We focus on the Internet version of the *Catalog* as available through GPO Access because it provides the most current documents.

USING THE *CATALOG*

To find federal publications on Alzheimer's disease, we turn to the *Catalog*. Our starting point is the GPO Access Web site maintained by the GPO (http://www.access.gpo.gov /su_docs/locators/chp/index.html). This site provides links to federal government documents and agencies as well as to other Web sites. Select the link for the *Catalog of United States Government Publications*.

We are presented with the user interface for a search engine that allows us to search the *Catalog* database. Figure 8.1 illustrates the appearance of that user interface. We may search the database in several ways: by keyword, keyword for titles available online, title, SuDoc Classification number, and several other means. The first three—keyword search (1), keyword search (online titles) (2), and title search (3)—are illustrated in Figure 8.1. We have specified a search for the text string "Alzheimer's Disease" (4) as a keyword search. Although the default is 40 document records, we have requested a maximum of 50 records (5). Note that this search engine uses Boolean operators as indicated by the examples (6) and follows most of the computer search conventions discussed in chapter 3.

Our search returns a list of 49 publications (7), as illustrated in Figure 8.2. On reviewing the list, item number 6 appears interesting. Information includes the title of

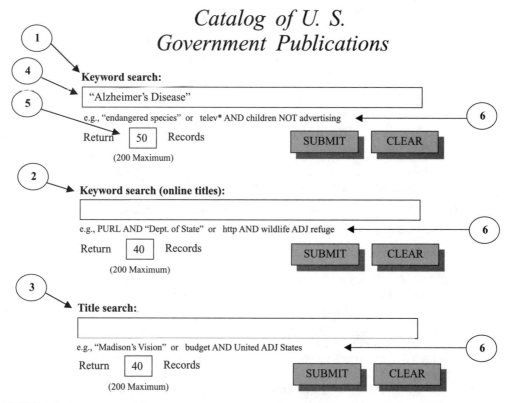

FIGURE 8.1. Initial user interface screen for online *Catalog of U. S. Government Publications* accessed through GPO Access.

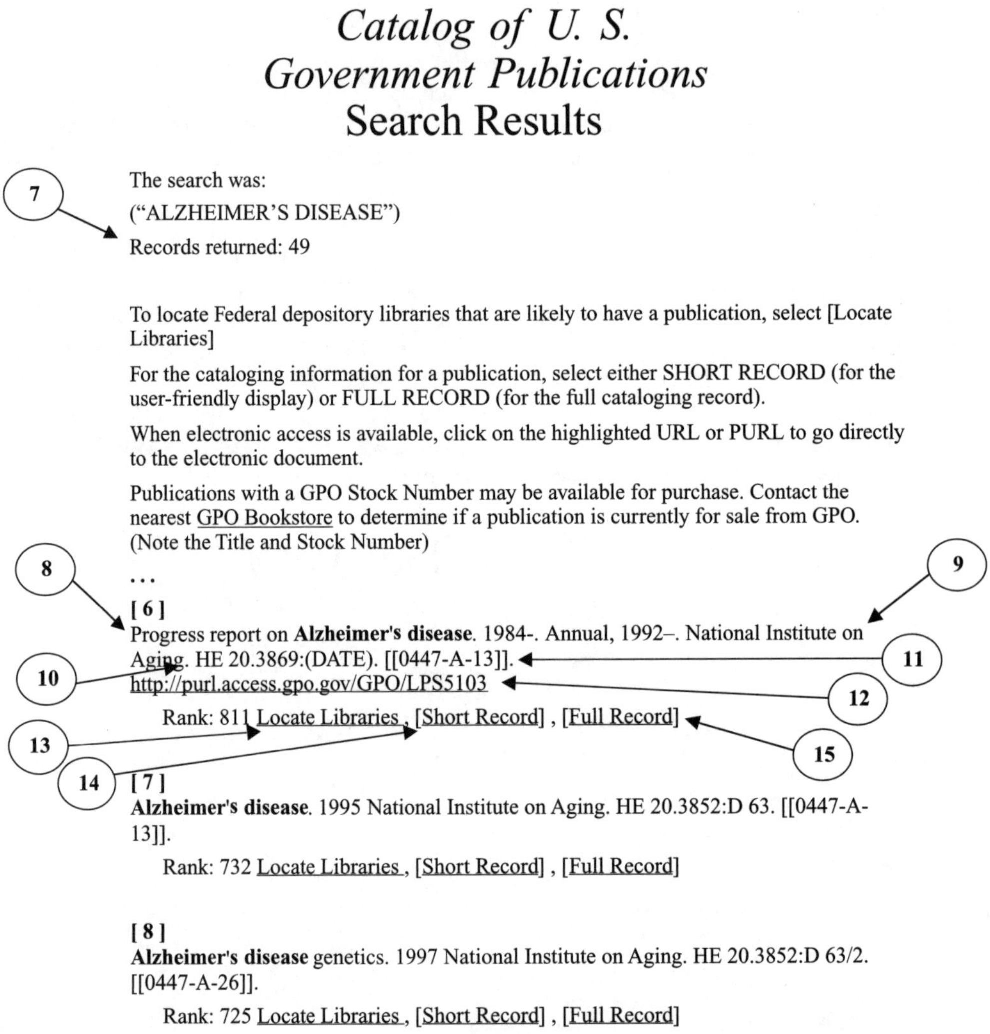

Catalog of U. S. Government Publications Search Results

⑦

The search was:
("ALZHEIMER'S DISEASE")
Records returned: 49

To locate Federal depository libraries that are likely to have a publication, select [Locate Libraries]

For the cataloging information for a publication, select either SHORT RECORD (for the user-friendly display) or FULL RECORD (for the full cataloging record).

When electronic access is available, click on the highlighted URL or PURL to go directly to the electronic document.

Publications with a GPO Stock Number may be available for purchase. Contact the nearest GPO Bookstore to determine if a publication is currently for sale from GPO. (Note the Title and Stock Number)

⑧ ⑨

...

[6]
Progress report on **Alzheimer's disease**. 1984-. Annual, 1992–. National Institute on Aging. HE 20.3869:(DATE). [[0447-A-13]].
⑩ ⑪
http://purl.access.gpo.gov/GPO/LPS5103
⑫

Rank: 811 Locate Libraries , [Short Record] , [Full Record]
⑬ ⑮
⑭ [7]
Alzheimer's disease. 1995 National Institute on Aging. HE 20.3852:D 63. [[0447-A-13]].

Rank: 732 Locate Libraries , [Short Record] , [Full Record]

[8]
Alzheimer's disease genetics. 1997 National Institute on Aging. HE 20.3852:D 63/2. [[0447-A-26]].

Rank: 725 Locate Libraries , [Short Record] , [Full Record]

FIGURE 8.2. Results of a search for information on Alzheimer's Disease using online *Catalog of U. S. Government Publications* accessed through GPO Access.

the document, *Progress Report on Alzheimer's Disease* (8), the issuing agency (9), the SuDoc Classification number (10), and the Depository Library series number (11). There are also hyperlinks to the Web site, which contains the text of this item (12), a locator for depository libraries that may have this document (13), a hyperlinked short record for the document (14), and a hyperlinked full record (15).

Examining the short record for this document, illustrated in Figure 8.3, we find that the document is an annual publication (16) first issued in 1984 (17) by the National Institute on Aging (18), an agency within the National Institutes of Health (19). We can tell from the final extension on the SuDoc number, 996, that this specific reference is to the 1996 edition (20). It is a part of Federal Depository Library series 0447-A-25 (21); those depository libraries that subscribe to this series of publications automatically

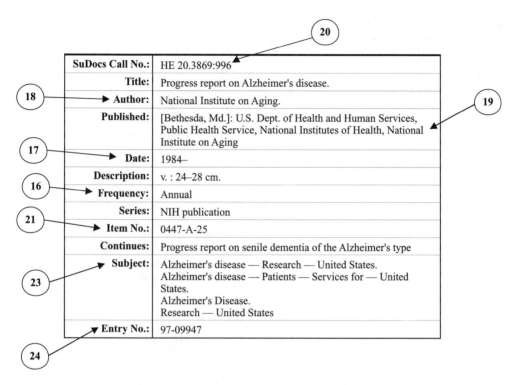

SuDocs Call No.:	HE 20.3869:996
Title:	Progress report on Alzheimer's disease.
Author:	National Institute on Aging.
Published:	[Bethesda, Md.]: U.S. Dept. of Health and Human Services, Public Health Service, National Institutes of Health, National Institute on Aging
Date:	1984–
Description:	v. : 24–28 cm.
Frequency:	Annual
Series:	NIH publication
Item No.:	0447-A-25
Continues:	Progress report on senile dementia of the Alzheimer's type
Subject:	Alzheimer's disease — Research — United States. Alzheimer's disease — Patients — Services for — United States. Alzheimer's Disease. Research — United States
Entry No.:	97-09947

FIGURE 8.3. Short record for item 6 in an online search of *Catalog of U. S. Government Publications* for Alzheimer's Disease.

receive a copy of this one. The entry number indicates that this was added to the database in 1997 as item 9947 (22). Four subject headings were used in the print version of the catalog's index (23). If we use the printed *MoCat* subject index, we would find this document indexed only under these four terms.

If we select the hyperlink for the Web page or the full record, we can access the document online. We continue by examining other records from our search results. Note that we can find publications on Alzheimer's disease issued by many agencies. Several examples are provided in Table 8.3. For each publication we have included the SuDoc number, the name of the issuing agency, and the title of the publication.

To find information published earlier than that included in the *Catalog,* we have to continue our search in the printed *MoCat*. We could also consult *MoCat* if we did not have Internet capabilities. We would have to rely on indexes that appear in the back of each monthly issue or annual cumulated index. (Annual cumulated indexes to the printed issues ended in 1995.) We may search by title, author, or title keyword in these indexes. Within each monthly issue, document entries are arranged by department and agency.

OTHER SOURCES

Publications are also issued by many government organizations in addition to those of the federal government. Many are not widely distributed and are therefore difficult to locate.

TABLE 8.3. Examples of Publications on Alzheimer's Disease From Various Agencies

SuDoc number	Issuing agency	Publication title
GA 1. 13: HEHS-98-16	General Accounting Office	*Alzheimer's disease estimates of prevalence in the United States.* (1998)
HE 23.3002: AL 9/11	Suncoast Gerontology Center for Administration on Aging	*Extending Alzheimer's support group intervention to ethnic minority caregivers.* (1989)
HE 20.6520: 19	Agency for Health Care Policy and Research	*Recognition and initial assessment of Alzheimer's disease and related dementias.* (1996)
HE 20.8102: B 73/4	National Institute of Mental Health	*Alzheimer's Disease.* (1994)
LC 33.10: 97-7	Library of Congress	*Alzheimer's Disease.* (1997)
Y 4.AG 4:HRG.104-517	Senate. Special Committee on Aging	*Alzheimer's Disease in a changing health care system: falling through the cracks.* (1996)

State Documents

You might want to investigate publications by state agencies, for example, to find out how a state is addressing a public policy issue. The Wisconsin Task Force on Alzheimer's Disease and Other Irreversible Dementias issued a *Final Report* (Wisconsin, 1987). Some states, such as Texas, maintain a depository program for its own publications, much like the federal depository program. Although many publications are now freely available on a state's Web page, the great number of state agencies can make your search for electronic publications difficult. In addition, some publications remain in paper only, may not be widely distributed, and can be difficult to locate outside of the state where they originated. Many states produce state-specific lists of their publications (often referred to as "checklists"), and some checklists can be searched on the Web. StateList, maintained jointly by the Documents and Law libraries of the University of Illinois at Urbana-Champaign, is a compilation of such electronic checklists. Coverage of many electronic checklists goes back only to the mid-1990s, and older material is indexed in the *Monthly Checklist of State Publications*, which ceased in 1994.

Unpublished Technical Reports

Each year thousands of technical, research, and development reports are prepared, many under the requirements of grants or contracts with a government agency. Similar to reports included in ERIC's *Resources in Education (RIE)* (see chapter 6), these publications often have limited distribution. The National Technical Information Service (NTIS), an agency of the U.S. Department of Commerce, acquires and indexes such items.

NTIS Product Search is a publicly available, online, electronic catalog covering 450,000 titles issued since 1990 and can be useful for locating these items. Some libraries receive selected documents indexed by NTIS on microfiche in the same way that some libraries receive ERIC microfiche indexed in *RIE*. Many items can also be ordered directly from NTIS or downloaded from the NTIS Web site.

International Organization Publications

Each year the United Nations (UN), its subsidiaries, and related agencies publish many hundreds of publications. These include information on population, children, the environment, trade, and many other topics. Like the U.S. federal government, the UN, through its Dag Hammarskjöld Library, has established a depository library system. There are approximately 400 UN depository libraries that receive international publications in countries around the world (United Nations Dag Hammarskjöld Library, 2001). In the United States these depository collections are often in large research university libraries such as at Florida State, Illinois, Northwestern, Stanford, University of California at Los Angeles, and Yale. Information about many UN publications is provided through the United Nations Bibliographic Information System (UNBIS), established in 1979. UNBIS contains information about documents acquired at either the Dag Hammarskjöld Library in New York City or at the United Nations Library in Geneva (United Nations Dag Hammarskjöld Library). UNBIS is also available to Internet users through UNBISnet. Like state documents and unpublished technical reports, publications of the UN and of other international agencies contain valuable information but may be difficult to obtain.

If you think that you will need to consult government publications, your first step should be to seek the assistance of a good reference librarian. Reference staff can help you negotiate the many databases, indexes, and Internet sources used to locate these elusive publications and can supply additional resources helpful to your search.

REFERENCES

McNeil, C. (1995). *Alzheimer's disease: Unraveling the mystery*. Washington, DC: National Institute on Aging.

Souêtré, E., Thwaites, R. M. A., and Yeardley, H. L. (1999). Economic impact of Alzheimer's disease in the United Kingdom: Cost of care and disease severity for non-institutionalised patients with Alzheimer's disease. *British Journal of Psychiatry, 174*, 51–55.

United Nations Dag Hammarskjöld Library. (n.d.). DHL Depository Library System. New York: United Nations. Retrieved March 11, 2002, from http://www.un.org/Depts/dhl/

U.S. Government Printing Office. (2002). *GPO fact sheet: The Government Printing Office—keeping America informed*. Retrieved February 3, 2002, from http://www.access.gpo.gov /public-affairs/5-99facts.html

U.S. National Institute of Neurological Disorders and Stroke. (2000). *Alzheimer's disease*. Washington, DC: NINDS, National Institutes of Health.

U.S. National Institute on Aging. (1995). *Alzheimer's disease fact sheet*. Washington, DC: National Institutes of Health.

van Reekum, R., Simard, M., & Cohen, T. (1999). The prediction and prevention of Alzheimer's disease—Toward a research agenda. *Journal of Psychiatry and Neuroscience, 24,* 413–430

Wisconsin Task Force on Alzheimer's Disease and Other Irreversible Dementias. (1987). *Final report of the Wisconsin task force on Alzheimer's disease and other irreversible dementias.* Madison, WI: Bureau on Aging, Department of Health and Social Services.

9 Psychological Tests and Measures

Sources Discussed

Mental Measurements Yearbook

Buros, O. K. (Ed.). *Mental measurements yearbook*. Highland Park, NJ: Gryphon Press. (1938). *1938 Mental measurements yearbook*. (1978). *Eighth mental measurements yearbook*.

Conoley, J. C., & Impara, J. C. (Eds.). (1995). *Twelfth mental measurements yearbook*. Lincoln, NE: Buros Institute of Mental Measurements, University of Nebraska.

Conoley, J. C., & Kramer, J. J. (Eds.). (1989). *Tenth mental measurements yearbook*. Lincoln, NE: Buros Institute of Mental Measurements, University of Nebraska.

Impara, J. C., & Plake, B. S. (Eds.). (1998). *Thirteenth mental measurements yearbook*. Lincoln, NE: Buros Institute of Mental Measurements, University of Nebraska.

Kramer, J. J., & Conoley, J. C. (Eds.). (1992). *Eleventh mental measurements yearbook*. Lincoln, NE: Buros Institute of Mental Measurements, University of Nebraska.

Mitchell. J. V., Jr. (Ed.). (1985). *Ninth mental measurements yearbook* (Vols. 1–2). Lincoln, NE: Buros Institute of Mental Measurements, University of Nebraska.

Plake, B. S., & Impara, J. C. (Eds.). (2001). *Fourteenth mental measurements yearbook*. Lincoln, NE: Buros Institute of Mental Measurements, University of Nebraska

Test Critiques

Keyser, D. J., & Sweetland, R. C. (Eds.). (1984–1988). *Test critiques* (Vols. 1–7). Kansas City, MO: Test Corporation of America.

Keyser, D. J., & Sweetland, R. C. (Eds.). (1991–1994). *Test critiques* (Vols. 8–10). Austin, TX: Pro-Ed.

Tests in Print

Buros, O. K. (Ed.). (1961). *Tests in print*. Highland Park, NJ: Gryphon Press.

Buros, O. K. (Ed.). (1974). *Tests in print II*. Highland Park, NJ: Gryphon Press.

Buros Institute of Mental Measurements. Buros: Complete Index. Retrieved January 2, 2002, from http://www.unl.edu/buros/index00.html

Mitchell, J. V. (Ed.). (1983). *Tests in print III*. Lincoln, NE: Buros Institute of Mental Measurements, University of Nebraska.

Murphy, L. L., Conoley, J. C., & Impara, J. C. (Eds.). (1994). *Tests in print IV* (Vols. 1–2). Lincoln, NE: Buros Institute of Mental Measurements, University of Nebraska.

Murphy, L. L., Impara, J. C., & Plake, B. S. (Eds.). (1999). *Tests in print V* (Vols. 1–2). Lincoln, NE: Buros Institute of Mental Measurements, University of Nebraska.

United States Educational Resources Information Center. Clearinghouse on Assessment and Evaluation. (1999). Ericae.net—test locator. Retrieved January 2, 2002, from http://ericae.net/testcol.htm

Directory of Unpublished Experimental Mental Measures
Educational Testing Service. (2002). *ETS test collection.* Retrieved February 24, 2002, from http://testcollection.ets.org

Goldman, B. A., & Busch, J. C. (Eds.). (1978–1982). *Directory of unpublished experimental mental measures* (Vols. 2–3). New York: Human Sciences Press.

Goldman, B. A., & Mitchell, D. F. (1990). *Directory of unpublished experimental mental measures* (Vol. 5). Dubuque, IA: William C. Brown.

Goldman, B. A., & Mitchell, D. F. (1995). *Directory of unpublished experimental mental measures* (Vol. 6). Washington, DC: American Psychological Association.

Goldman, B. A., & Mitchell, D. F. (2002). *Directory of unpublished experimental mental measures* (Vol. 8). Washington, DC: American Psychological Association.

Goldman, B. A., Mitchell, D. F., & Egelson, P. E. (1997). *Directory of unpublished experimental mental measures* (Vol. 7). Washington, DC: American Psychological Association.

Goldman, B. A., & Osborne, W. L. (1985). *Directory of unpublished experimental mental measures* (Vol. 4). New York: Human Sciences Press.

Goldman, B. A., & Saunders, J. L. (Eds.). (1974). *Directory of unpublished experimental mental measures* (Vol. 1). New York: Behavioral Publications.

Maddox, T. (1997). *Tests: A comprehensive reference for assessments in psychology, education, and business* (4th ed.). Austin, TX: Pro-Ed.

NEED FOR INFORMATION ON TESTS AND MEASURES

PSYCHOLOGISTS NEED information about tests in many situations. For example, school psychologists evaluate children referred by classroom teachers who observe learning difficulties. School psychologists must know which of the many tests is most appropriate to use in the particular situation. They must know how to administer, score, and interpret test results; they must know the limits of the test; and they must be able to make recommendations to the teacher. School psychologists learn much about testing in graduate school but must also be able to continue learning as new measures become available. Similarly, vocational counselors use tests to gather information about interests, aptitudes, and skills to assist individuals in exploring career options. The counselors must be familiar with the strengths and weaknesses of various tests for different situations.

Researchers may use tests to measure abilities, achievement, attitudes, behaviors, dispositions, and other variables relevant to a particular hypothesis. They might use an existing measure or construct a new one. A new measure, however, might lack reliability or validity. In addition, comparison with prior research might be difficult. If searching for an existing measure, researchers need to know about available measures that might be appropriate for a given situation.

Psychology students may need information about a test. You might be enrolled in a course on psychological testing in which you are required to learn about a variety of measures. You might be writing a paper on a topic that relies heavily on use of one or several tests; you need to understand the assumptions, theory, structure, limitations, and interpretation of the measures used in the research. You might be designing a research project—senior honors project, master's thesis, doctoral dissertation—and need to select a test to measure a particular construct relevant to your hypothesis.

Psychological tests and measures of one type or another are used frequently in research. They represent particular ways of operationalizing psychological concepts to enable collection of data about them. Different operational definitions of the same concept lead to different measurement strategies. A psychological construct, such as personality, is defined in many ways.

CHAPTER EXAMPLE: PERSONALITY TESTING

What is personality? Although definitions differ, there is consensus that it is a complex hypothetical construct that describes an individual person. It is the collection of ways of behaving, feeling, and thinking that are typical for a person and that differentiate that person from all other persons.

How many personality dimensions are there? There are many theoretical approaches to understanding personality. They start with different assumptions and focus on varied aspects of individual differences. As a result, each approach has developed a different number and set of dimensions. Theories may be grouped broadly into four basic approaches: psychodynamic (e.g., Freud, 1924; Jung, 1926), behavioral (e.g., Bandura, 1977; Mischel, 1973; Rotter, 1982), humanistic (e.g., Maslow, 1970; Rogers, 1961), and biological (e.g., Eysenck, 1967). Some psychologists have attempted to identify the most basic dimensions that form the core of personality. McCrae and Costa (1987, 1997) suggested a five-factor model of personality. They suggested that most personality traits are derived from five higher-order ones. These have become known as the Big Five: extraversion (positive emotionality), neuroticism (negative emotionality), openness to experience, agreeableness, and conscientiousness (constraint). The five-factor theory became the key approach to personality structure in the 1990s.

How is personality measured? Just as there are different theoretical approaches and operationalizations of personality, the construct has been assessed in many ways. For example, the Rorschach Inkblot Test asks respondents to describe what they see in a series of inkblots (Rorschach, 1942). It is a projective test that was derived from a psychodynamic perspective on personality. The test was developed based on the belief that the roots of personality are to be found in the unconscious and that by asking subjects to describe what they see in ambiguous stimuli, the test can tap the unconscious to reveal aspects of personality. In contrast the Minnesota Multiphasic Personality Inventory (MMPI) asks subjects to respond to a series of 567 true-or-false questions (Butcher, Dahlstrom, Graham, Tellegen, & Kaemmer, 1989). Items are divided into a series of 10 scales designed to describe different dimensions of personality (e.g., depression, hysteria, paranoia). Responses to the questions are compared with responses of other persons who have been determined to have these defined personality characteristics; this is known as the empirical keying method. The result is a profile of scores for an individual on a set of personality dimensions. The MMPI is an empirically derived test. The Rorschach Inkblot Test and the MMPI are radically different and yield quite different descriptions of an individual's personality.

Selecting one or another of these tests has a critical impact on findings that emerge from your research. As a researcher you must be aware of the influence of different measures on outcomes you are likely to find. As a reader of research you must be aware of the influence of a measurement strategy on a piece of research.

To illustrate the process of finding information about psychological tests and measures, we selected the Hogan Personality Inventory (HPI). Published in 1995, this revised edition of the HPI is a measure of normal personality and is designed for use in personnel selection, individual assessment, and career-related decision making (Hogan & Hogan, 1995). The HPI has seven primary scale scores, six occupational scale scores, and a validity scale score. The authors indicated that the form was revised to align more closely with the five-factor theory. John's (1990) data indicated that the dimensionality of the HPI aligns with the five-factor theory.

PUBLISHED TESTS

The *Mental Measurements Yearbooks* (*MMY*) and its companion publication *Tests in Print* (*TIP*) provide the most extensive coverage of published standardized tests commercially available in the English-speaking world. The first eight *MMY* volumes, published from 1938 through 1978, were edited by Oscar Krisen Buros with the assistance of Luella Buros. The volumes are still widely known simply as Buros. Contrary to the title, *MMY* volumes are not published every year. Until the ninth edition, they appeared at 6- to 10-year intervals. Beginning in 1988 new editions appeared more frequently, generally about every 3 years, and were updated by a paper supplement during intervening years.

The *MMY* volumes provide detailed information on published tests for use with English-speaking subjects and critical reviews of most of those tests. Volumes also provide extensive bibliographies of references to tests listed in *MMY*, although wider availability of bibliographic databases such as PsycINFO (see chapter 5) led to the decision to discontinue this feature with the 14th *MMY*. Older *MMY* editions also list and cite reviews of books on testing and measurement. The *MMY* editions supplement each other, with succeeding editions including only new tests, substantially revised tests, and new information about previously reviewed tests. The 14th *MMY* (published in 2001) contains information on 430 new and revised tests issued after publication of the 13th *MMY*. It also provides reviews for tests that appeared in the previous *MMY*. In total, the 14th *MMY* contains 802 original reviews by 461 different authors (Plake & Impara, 2001, p. x).

O. K. Buros began compiling *TIP* in 1961. New editions were published at infrequent intervals, the most recent being *Tests in Print V* (*TIP5*) in 1999. According to its introduction *TIP5* contained 2,939 test entries. Beginning with *TIP5* the Buros Institute planned a new edition every 5 years. *TIP* and *MMY* volumes complement each other. The strength of *MMY* lies in its descriptive information on tests, extensive retrospective reference lists, and critical reviews. *TIP* provides descriptive information for tests currently available for purchase and acts as an index to tests and their reviews that appear in the *MMY* volumes. For example, *TIP5* is a comprehensive index to tests that are still commercially available for purchase and that were reviewed in the first 13 *MMY* editions. (An important point to remember, however, is that out-of-print tests do not appear in a *TIP* volume, although *TIP* does have a separate list of tests newly out of print since the preceding edition.)

INDEXES TO INFORMATION ABOUT PUBLISHED TESTS

Although you can search each *MMY* edition to locate test reviews, there are several cumulative indexes to the editions. One approach is to use the Buros Institute's Web site, which has a cumulative title index to all tests included in the *MMY* editions since *MMY9*, published in 1985. In addition, the Web site indexes these tests under 19 broad subject areas. These title and subject category indexes provide a citation to the *MMY* edition in which a test's review was published. For a fee you can also order copies of many test reviews directly from the Buros Institute.

A similar test review locator is provided by the Educational Resources Information Center (ERIC) Clearinghouse on Assessment and Evaluation and is helpful for searching by a test's title. This Web site is maintained cooperatively by the Educational Testing Service (ETS), the Buros Institute, George Washington University, and the test publisher Pro-Ed. One of the site's features is the ability to search for test reviews appearing in the *MMY* publications and in the *Test Critiques* series published by Pro-Ed (described in the later section "Other Information Sources for Published Tests.") You can also search using partial words from the title. For example, entering *hog* and *person* in the search query boxes retrieves citations to reviews of the HPI (both editions) as well as to the Hogan Personnel Selection Series. In addition to searches for test reviews, this Web site allows you to search for test publisher information.

Another approach is to use the most recent edition of *TIP*, which provides more complete indexing for tests than the two preceding sources. Although its primary function is to provide purchasing information for tests (even those not yet reviewed in *MMY* volumes), *TIP* also acts as an index to the contents of all preceding *MMY* editions. *TIP5* volumes contained several indexes: Index of Titles, Index of Acronyms, Classified Subject Index, Publishers Directory and Index, Index of Names, and a Score Index. The Index of Titles listed all tests in *TIP5* and out-of-print tests that appeared in *TIP4*, *MMY12*, and *MMY13*. Because the Hogan Personality Inventory is known by the acronym HPI, we can locate it by using the Index of Acronyms. The test was also listed alphabetically in the Index of Names under its authors, Robert Hogan and Joyce Hogan. The Classified Subject Index lists each test and the population for which it is intended under the following 19 broad categories:

1. Achievement
2. Behavior assessment
3. Developmental
4. Education
5. English and language
6. Fine arts
7. Foreign languages
8. Intelligence and general aptitude
9. Mathematics
10. Miscellaneous
11. Multiaptitude batteries (a category discontinued after publication of *TIP5*)
12. Neuropsychological
13. Personality
14. Reading
15. Science
16. Sensory-motor
17. Social studies

18. Speech and hearing

19. Vocations

In this case the HPI is listed under the category of Personality. Had we not known about the HPI, we could have consulted the Classified Subject Index and found information about numerous personality tests. By using the Score Index, we can locate tests in *TIP5* that measure specific variables or particular attributes (e.g., self-direction, leadership). The Publishers Directory and Index lists *TIP5* test numbers by their publishers and includes publishers' addresses, phone numbers, e-mail addresses, and Web site URLs. In addition, *TIP5* has a separate index of tests newly out of print since their inclusion in *TIP4*, *MMY12*, and *MMY13* and an Index of Names to all test reviewers whose reviews were published in all preceding *MMY* editions. All indexes provide test numbers (not page numbers) by which tests are listed sequentially in the body of *TIP5* or *MMY* editions. Using *TIP* as an index to *MMY* test reviews has two limitations. *TIP* includes only tests still available from publishers, and it is published less frequently than *MMY* editions. Therefore, if you are searching for a test published after a *TIP* edition (for example, in 1999), it will not be included in the 5th edition of the *TIP*, published in 1998, but may be included in the 15th edition of the *MMY*, published in 2001. A good rule of thumb is to search the *TIP* indexes first, unless the test you seek was published more recently than the newest *TIP*; in that case start with the most recent *MMY* edition.

USING THE *MENTAL MEASUREMENTS YEARBOOK*

The revised version of the HPI was published in 1995. By using all three of the indexes just described, we can locate its review in the 13th edition of the *MMY* as test entry 138 (1), as illustrated in Figure 9.1. The test title appears in boldface (2), followed by a general statement about the purpose of the test (3). The review also provides information on the groups for which the test is intended (4); the publication dates for forms, documentation, and a test's editions (5); and an acronym (6) by which the test is often identified. One test may include many scores, and these are provided (7). The entry also provides administration information, for example, if the test can be administered individually or by group and the estimated time needed (8). Price information as of the time of publication is indicated (9). Author(s) and publisher(s) names are also included (10). Cross-references can be useful for locating reviews of previous versions of the test as they appeared in preceding *MMY* editions (11). In this case *TIP4* contains seven references about the test, and the 10th *MMY* has two reviews of an earlier version of the HPI under test entry 140. A list of references to published literature about the test follows (12), although this feature no longer appears in *MMY* volumes beginning with the 14th edition. Two critical reviews follow (13), including the names and credentials of the reviewers; the first is excerpted in Figure 9.1. Other information provided in test entries can include the availability of alternate versions of a test (for example, publication in foreign languages or in Braille), restrictions on distribution, and other notes relevant to use or interpretation of the measure (although these elements do not pertain to the HPI).

MMY volumes contain six indexes that supplement the title/entry number arrangement, some of which parallel their *TIP* equivalents: Index of Titles, Index of Acronyms, Classified Subject Index, Publishers Directory and Index, Index of Names (for test authors, test reviewers, and reference authors), and Score Index. The Index of Titles is useful for tests that

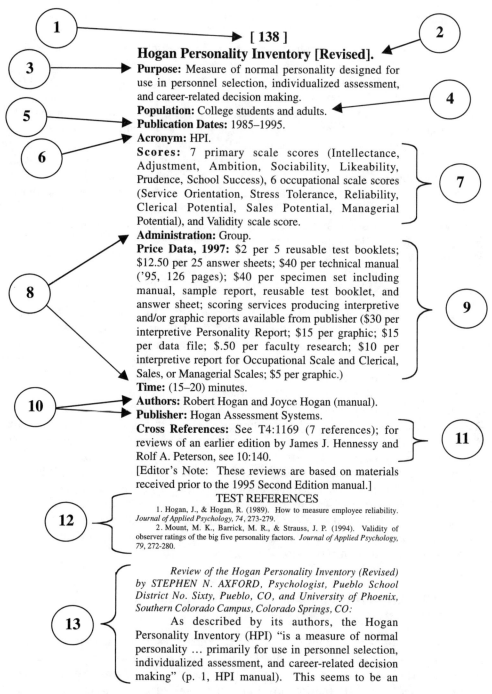

[138]

Hogan Personality Inventory [Revised].

Purpose: Measure of normal personality designed for use in personnel selection, individualized assessment, and career-related decision making.

Population: College students and adults.

Publication Dates: 1985–1995.

Acronym: HPI.

Scores: 7 primary scale scores (Intellectance, Adjustment, Ambition, Sociability, Likeability, Prudence, School Success), 6 occupational scale scores (Service Orientation, Stress Tolerance, Reliability, Clerical Potential, Sales Potential, Managerial Potential), and Validity scale score.

Administration: Group.

Price Data, 1997: $2 per 5 reusable test booklets; $12.50 per 25 answer sheets; $40 per technical manual ('95, 126 pages); $40 per specimen set including manual, sample report, reusable test booklet, and answer sheet; scoring services producing interpretive and/or graphic reports available from publisher ($30 per interpretive Personality Report; $15 per graphic; $15 per data file; $.50 per faculty research; $10 per interpretive report for Occupational Scale and Clerical, Sales, or Managerial Scales; $5 per graphic.)

Time: (15–20) minutes.

Authors: Robert Hogan and Joyce Hogan (manual).

Publisher: Hogan Assessment Systems.

Cross References: See T4:1169 (7 references); for reviews of an earlier edition by James J. Hennessy and Rolf A. Peterson, see 10:140.

[Editor's Note: These reviews are based on materials received prior to the 1995 Second Edition manual.]

TEST REFERENCES

1. Hogan, J., & Hogan, R. (1989). How to measure employee reliability. *Journal of Applied Psychology, 74*, 273-279.
2. Mount, M. K., Barrick, M. R., & Strauss, J. P. (1994). Validity of observer ratings of the big five personality factors. *Journal of Applied Psychology, 79*, 272-280.

Review of the Hogan Personality Inventory (Revised) by STEPHEN N. AXFORD, Psychologist, Pueblo School District No. Sixty, Pueblo, CO, and University of Phoenix, Southern Colorado Campus, Colorado Springs, CO:

As described by its authors, the Hogan Personality Inventory (HPI) "is a measure of normal personality ... primarily for use in personnel selection, individualized assessment, and career-related decision making" (p. 1, HPI manual). This seems to be an

FIGURE 9.1. Example of a test entry of the Hogan Personality Inventory. From *The Thirteenth Annual Mental Measurements Yearbook* (pp. 483–484), B. S. Plake & J. C. Impara (Eds.), 1998, Lincoln, NE: Buros Institute of Mental Measurements. Copyright 1998 by Buros Institute of Mental Measurements. Reprinted with permission.

change titles between *MMY* editions or that are commonly known or referred to in professional literature by alternate titles. Beginning with the 14th *MMY* there is also a listing of tests that were not reviewed because they lacked sufficient technical documentation.

The *MMY* is also available as an electronic product produced by SilverPlatter Information/Ovid Technologies. This is a comprehensive search product that includes the contents of all *MMY* editions from the ninth to the most recent. It has several advantages over the printed *MMY* and *TIP* volumes and the Web-based indexes already described. This version is updated every 6 months, making it considerably more current than the alternatives, and replaces descriptions and reviews when new ones are produced. It allows multiple field searching as well as browsing of the standard indexes (by author, title, publisher, and other criteria). For example, if you want to find a test that contains two distinct scores, you can search for *ambition* **AND** *manager** (to search for *managerial*, *managers*, and so on) to find tests that measure both attributes. Another feature is the ability to search for terms in the reviews. For example, a title search locates not only reviews of that test but also locates any review in which that test title is mentioned. This is convenient for locating reviews in which several tests are compared.

OTHER INFORMATION SOURCES FOR PUBLISHED TESTS

Although the Buros series is the most comprehensive tool covering published tests, there are several others worth mentioning. *Test Critiques* was published in 10 volumes from 1984 to 1995. Each volume contained approximately 100 test reviews. Tests and their reviews are arranged by test title, with indexes by title, publishers, test authors and reviewers, and subject. Compared with the *MMY*, *Test Critiques* provides less descriptive information about tests and cites fewer studies in reference lists. However, reviews are usually longer, sometimes employ illustrative charts and tables, and provide more technical data associated with each test. The greatest drawback of this series is that it is no longer published; its utility decreases as the tests it contains are revised or no longer published.

Tests is a directory of approximately 2,000 published English-language tests. The measures are categorized under the areas of psychology, education, and business, with each broad area further subdivided, for a total of 89 subcategories. Although *Tests* does not contain reviews, each measure is accompanied by a brief description, the intended use, cost, and availability. It is designed as a quick guide to finding tests meeting a specific need. Among its indexes are those by publisher, test title, author, tests available in foreign languages, and computer-scored tests.

INFORMATION SOURCES FOR UNPUBLISHED TESTS AND MEASURES

Thousands of tests, questionnaires, and other measuring instruments created by researchers are not commercially available. Often they are mentioned only briefly in a research report or presented in an article or book. You may find locating such measuring instruments difficult. Information on their technical adequacy (reliability, validity, norms, and so forth) may be scanty, if available at all. Since the 1960s several sources that attempt to provide access to these various materials have been published.

The *Directory of Unpublished Experimental Mental Measures (Directory)* lists unpublished tests appearing in many psychology and related journals. At present there are eight volumes of the *Directory*, covering tests available in journal articles published in 1970 (Vol. 1), 1971–1972 (Vol. 2), 1973–1974 (Vol. 3), 1974–1980 (Vol. 4), 1981–1985 (Vol. 5), 1986–1990 (Vol. 6), 1991–1995 (Vol. 7), and 1996–2000 (Vol. 8). Included in the *Directory* is a brief description of each measure and a reference to the journal in which test-related information appears. Tests are grouped by general type (attitudes, personality, and so forth), and a cumulative subject index is included.

Several other sources provide information of possible interest, although some have not been updated and therefore are not helpful for locating very recent tests. In *Measures for Psychological Assessment*, Chun, Cobb, and French (1975) compiled 3,000 references to articles in social science journals that reported the use of various tests and measures. The *Sourcebook of Mental Health Measures* (Comrey, Backer, & Glaser, 1973) complements their efforts by listing and abstracting 1,100 tests, questionnaires, rating scales, and inventories not included by Chun et al. *Tests and Measurements in Child Development* (Johnson, 1976; Johnson & Bommarito, 1971) is limited to research on children and provides a more focused approach. *Handbook 1* (Johnson & Bommarito, 1971) covers tests reported before 1965 for infants through children 12 years old. *Handbook II* (Johnson, 1976) expands coverage to infancy through age 18 years and includes materials reported from 1966 through 1974. Descriptive information is provided for each measure, accompanied by the source of the information.

Several sources exist in the area of attitude measurement. A three-volume series originally published under the auspices of the Survey Research Center at the University of Michigan (Robinson, Athanasiou, & Head, 1969; Robinson, Shaver, & Wrightsman, 1991, 1999) covers approximately 300 attitude scales. These volumes provide descriptive information, brief evaluative information, sources, and either sample items or the whole measure. Shaw and Wright (1967) present approximately 175 attitude measurement scales, including the full test, scoring, and background information.

These sources supplement *MMY* by providing information on a variety of unpublished measures. Other sources include both published and unpublished measures. The *ETS Test Collection* catalog includes information about unpublished research instruments in periodicals, commercially available tests and questionnaires, and approximately 1,000 measures in the ETS's *Tests in Microfiche* collection. The tests in this catalog are not limited to current materials. Some tests, including those that are part of *Tests in Microfiche*, may be ordered online from ETS for a fee. The *ETS Test Collection* Web site permits searching by test author, title, publisher, words in the abstract, and many other criteria.

An International Directory of Spatial Tests (Eliot & Smith, 1983) includes information about 400 pencil-and-paper tests that measure spatial ability, such as figural rotations, mazes, and visual memory tests. Published, out-of-print, and unpublished measures are included. *Measuring Health* (McDowell & Newell, 1996) includes evaluations of more than 80 tests, many accompanied by sample items, and is of interest to those working in health psychology. *Women and Women's Issues* (Beere, 1979) is a compilation of information on 235 instruments and is, in part, supplemented by 211 instruments included in *Gender Roles: A Handbook of Tests and Measures* (Beere, 1990). These two books include information about unpublished and published measures available through the end of 1977 and mid-1988, respectively. *Handbook of Sexuality-Related Measures* (Davis, Yarber, Bauserman, Schreer, & Davis, 1998) discusses approximately 200 commercially available tests developed by individual researchers, and it reprints questions selected from many of them.

YOUR RESPONSIBILITY AS A USER OF TESTS AND MEASURES

Using these sources, you can search for information about tests and measures relevant to your research, papers, and courses. There are several caveats you should keep in mind if you are planning to go beyond looking at test reviews and use published or unpublished tests.

- Most tests are copyrighted, even those included in journal articles and books. Therefore, you cannot modify questions or reproduce a test without permission from the copyright holder.

- Many test publishers impose restrictions on who can purchase and use their testing products. There are several reasons for this in addition to copyright. The misuse of a measure may compromise the integrity of the test itself. Most published tests are intended to be administered and interpreted by those qualified to do so, for example, a psychologist, social worker, or counselor. Publishers' catalogs or their Web sites provide more information about the categories of test purchasers and what tests each user category may purchase.

- Because of the sensitivity of some published psychological tests and measures, you may not find the measures in your college library. Some libraries, as a matter of policy, do not maintain a collection of psychological tests. In many cases you will need to contact a psychologist in a department of psychology, counseling center, or other facility at your college to discuss the availability and appropriateness of a test you wish to examine.

Using tests and conducting surveys should not be undertaken lightly. Most campuses have a human subjects review process to which all such research—including that undertaken by students—must be submitted. To provide guidelines for use of tests, *Standards for Educational and Psychological Testing* (1999) was developed jointly by the American Psychological Association, the American Educational Research Association, and the National Council on Measurement in Education. There are many other standards concerning the use of tests developed by professional groups that address specific testing environments, such as educational and workplace settings.

REFERENCES

American Educational Research Association. (1999). *Standards for educational and psychological testing*. Washington, DC: Author.

Bandura, A. (1977). *Social learning theory*. Englewood Cliffs, NJ: Prentice-Hall.

Beere, C. A. (1979). *Women and women's issues: A handbook of tests and measures*. San Francisco: Jossey-Bass.

Beere, C. A. (1990). *Gender roles: A handbook of tests and measures*. New York: Greenwood.

Butcher, J. N., Dahlstrom, W., Graham, J., Tellegen, A., & Kaemmer, B. (1989). *Manual for administering and scoring the MMPI–2*. Minneapolis, MN: University of Minnesota Press.

Chun, K., Cobb, S., & French, J. R. P. (1975). *Measures for psychological assessment*. Ann Arbor, MI: Survey Research Center.

Comrey, A. L., Backer, T. E., & Glaser, E. M. (1973). *A sourcebook of mental health measures*. Los Angeles: Human Interaction Research Institute.

Davis, C. M., Yarber, W. L., Bauserman, R., Schreer, G., & Davis, S. L. (1998). *Handbook of sexuality-related measures*. Thousand Oaks, CA: Sage Publications.

Eliot, J., & Smith, I. M. (1983). *An international directory of spatial tests*. Windsor, Berkshire, England: NFER-Nelson.

Eysenck, H. J. (1967). *The biological basis of personality*. Springfield, IL: Thomas.

Freud, S. (1924). *A general introduction to psychoanalysis*. New York: Boni & Liveright.

Hogan, R., & Hogan, J. (1995). *Hogan personality inventory* (Rev. ed.). Tulsa, OK: Hogan Assessment Systems.

John, O. (1990). The "big five" factor taxonomy: Dimensions of personality in the natural language and in questionnaires. In L. A. Pervin (Ed.), *Handbook of personality: Theory and research* (pp. 66–100). New York: Guilford Press.

Johnson, O. G. (Ed.). (1976). *Tests and measurements in child development: Handbook II* (Vols. 1–2). San Francisco: Jossey-Bass.

Johnson, O. G., & Bommarito, J. W. (Eds.). (1971). *Tests and measurements in child development: Handbook I*. San Francisco: Jossey-Bass.

Jung, C. G. (1926). *Psychological types*. New York: Harcourt, Brace & Co.

Maslow, A. H. (1970). *Motivation and personality*. New York: Harper & Row.

McCrae, R. R., & Costa, P. T., Jr. (1987). Validation of the five-factor model of personality across instruments and observers. *Journal of Personality and Social Psychology, 52*, 81–90.

McCrae, R. R., & Costa, P. T., Jr. (1997). Personality trait structure as a human universal. *American Psychologist, 52*, 509–516.

McDowell, I., & Newell, C. (1996). *Measuring health: A guide to rating scales and questionnaires*. New York: Oxford University Press.

Mischel, W. (1973). Toward a cognitive social learning conceptualization of personality. *Psychological Review, 80*, 252–283.

Plake, B. S., & Impara, J. C. (Eds.). (2001). *Fourteenth mental measurements yearbook*. Lincoln, NE: Buros Institute of Mental Measurements, University of Nebraska.

Robinson, J. P., Athanasiou, R., & Head, K. B. (1969). *Measures of occupational attitudes and occupational characteristics*. Ann Arbor, MI: Survey Research Center.

Robinson, J. P., Shaver, P. R., & Wrightsman, L. S. (1991). *Measures of personality and social psychological attitudes*. San Diego, CA: Academic Press.

Robinson, J. P., Shaver, P. R., & Wrightsman, L. S. (1999). *Measures of political attitudes* (2nd ed.). San Diego, CA: Academic Press.

Rogers, C. R. (1961). *On becoming a person: A therapist's view of psychotherapy*. Boston: Houghton Mifflin.

Rorschach, H. (1942). *Psychodiagnostics: A diagnostic test based on perception*. Berne, Switzerland: Huber.

Rotter, J. B. (1982). *The development and application of social learning theory*. New York: Praeger.

Shaw, M. E., & Wright, J. M. (1967). *Scales for the measurement of attitudes*. New York: McGraw-Hill.

10 Miscellaneous Sources

IN PREVIOUS chapters we presented various sources you can use to find information about a topic in psychology. We explored subject and citation searching, commercial publishers, and government sources of information. Tools such as PsycINFO and *Psychological Abstracts* enable you to conduct a retrospective literature search to locate information on a particular subject.

The sources discussed in this chapter serve a different purpose. They can broaden your knowledge of an area of psychology. Biographical information allows you to find out about the people in a field. Doctoral dissertations are an important source of unpublished original research. Book reviews provide informed opinions on the potential usefulness and reliability of new books.

Suppose that you are presented with an opportunity to meet a well-known person who will visit your campus as a guest speaker. In the afternoon before the presentation you and a group of others will have an opportunity to talk with the speaker. You would like to prepare for this seminar so you can be involved intelligently in the discussion. What information might you seek? After you use the sources discussed in earlier chapters to find research reports in journals, handbooks, and books written by the speaker, you will need to supplement these. You probably want to gather some biographical information on the individual. If the speaker completed a doctorate, maybe information on the doctoral dissertation will be useful. If the person has written one or more books, the reviews of those books might be interesting as an indicator of the author's stature in the field and as a perspective on that author's work.

CHAPTER EXAMPLE: LEADERSHIP AND WARREN BENNIS

In this chapter we focus on leadership to illustrate our searches. Leadership requires getting other people to achieve organization goals. Leading involves creating a vision for the future, developing a strategy to achieve that vision, communicating the vision, and enlisting the support of others to achieve the vision. Leadership brings about change in organizations; it requires motivation and participation of others.

Like many other topics in psychology, leadership is a complex and multifaceted one. Why are some people more successful than others as leaders? What do successful leaders do? Are leaders born, or can they be developed? Researchers have studied many different aspects of leadership.

Some researchers have focused on personality traits (Stogdill, 1948). Personality traits such as dominance, self-confidence, and achievement drive have been reported as characteristic of leaders (Bass, 1981). Researchers have tried to identify those dimensions of personality common to leaders that differentiate successful leaders from unsuccessful leaders or from followers (e.g., Kenny & Zaccaro, 1983).

The behavior of leaders has also been an important consideration. The Ohio State Studies (e.g., Fleishman, 1953; Shartle, 1950; Stogdill, 1957) identified two key dimensions of leader behavior: consideration (the extent to which the leader exhibits concern for the welfare of the followers) and initiating structure (the extent to which the leader initiates, defines, and organizes activity in a group). These studies laid the groundwork for subsequent behavioral approaches such as the Leadership Grid (Blake and Mouton, 1964) and the Coaching Behavior Assessment System (Curtis, Smith, & Smoll, 1979). Fiedler's (1971) contingency model focused on interaction between the leader and the situation, whereas the situational theory of Hersey and Blanchard (1969) addressed the interaction between a leader's style choice and maturity of the follower.

In recent years attention has increasingly been on dimensions such as empowerment and values of leaders. As organizations have undergone downsizing and reorganizing there has been increased attention to empowering workers and providing them with the information and authority they need to do their jobs. Leaders are learning to empower their followers (Quinn & Spreitzer, 1997). Authors such as Kotter (1996) have focused on change and the leader's role in directing the organization—developing and communicating the vision, building support for the change, and so forth. Inquiring about what is most important in being successful as a leader, Kouzes and Posner (1995) wrote about the importance of having vision, sharing power, fostering collaboration, setting an example for others to follow, having credibility, and encouraging others.

One of the premier writers on leadership during the past two decades has been Warren G. Bennis. He has written about leadership topics such as self-knowledge, knowing others, and values (Bennis, 1989a) and the importance of collaboration and teams (Bennis, 1997b). His credits include *Managing People Is Like Herding Cats* (Bennis, 1997a), *On Becoming a Leader* (Bennis, 1989a), *Organizing Genius* (Bennis, 1997b), and *Why Leaders Can't Lead* (Bennis, 1989b). Suppose that Mr. Bennis is to be your guest speaker and you would like to learn more about him. In the remainder of this chapter we describe sources that enable us to find out more about Mr. Bennis, his work, and his influence on research on leadership.

BIOGRAPHICAL INFORMATION

Sources Discussed

American Psychological Association. (1948–present). *Directory of the American Psychological Association*. Washington, DC: Author.

American Psychological Association. (1967–present). *American Psychological Association membership register*. Washington, DC: Author.

Contemporary authors. (1962–present). Detroit, MI: Gale.

Who's who. (1899–present). Chicago, IL: Marquis Who's Who.

Who's who in America. (1899–present). Chicago, IL: Marquis Who's Who.

Who's who in the east. (1969–present). Chicago, IL: Marquis Who's Who.

Directories

Biographical directories serve many purposes. They provide current mailing addresses, list academic credentials, and indicate recent publications. There are many biographical directories, each providing a different type of information and scope of coverage.

The primary purpose of the *Directory of the American Psychological Association (Directory)* is to provide brief biographical data on APA members. Questionnaires sent to APA members every few years solicit data. The *American Psychological Association Membership Register*, published annually, provides current affiliation and location information. There are several limitations to these sources. Only persons who are APA members are included, and the data are only as good as that provided by the members.

Another series of biographical directories is produced by Marquis Who's Who. This series includes a variety of editions: *Who's Who in America, Who's Who in the East,* and many others. These provide biographical information, as illustrated for Warren Bennis in Figure 10.1, as it appeared in the 2000–2001 edition of *Who's Who in America.* The

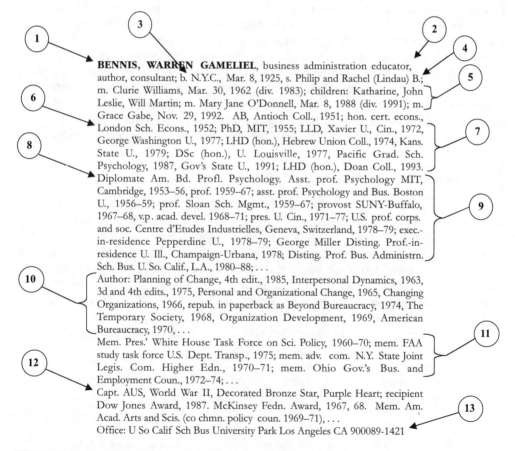

FIGURE 10.1. Portions of an entry for Warren Bennis in *Who's Who in America.* From *Who's Who in America, 2000,* (54th. ed., vol. 1), 2000, Chicago, IL: Marquis Publishing Group. Copyright 2000 by Marquis Publishing Group. Reprinted with permission.

entry starts with the full name of the biographee (1), his primary professional roles (2), location and date of birth (3), parents (4), and his family (5). His academic background includes earned degrees from Antioch College and Massachusetts Institute of Technology (MIT) (6) and honorary degrees from institutions such as Xavier and George Washington Universities (7). He is a diplomate (that is, certified as a specialist) of the American Board of Professional Psychology (8). The following section provides his work history (9), starting with a position as assistant professor of psychology at MIT from 1953 through 1956. His scholarly work (10) includes authorship of numerous books. He served on many boards and commissions (11), and he received the Bronze Star and Purple Heart while in the U.S. Army during World War II (12). The entry closes with his most recently known business address (13).

Another source to consider is *Contemporary Authors (CA)*. It is a guide to writers who have authored works of fiction and nonfiction. Like the *Who's Who* series, *CA* is a general publication covering all disciplines. It can be an important resource if the psychologist whose biography you seek has published several books. In addition to awards received, personal information, and career information, *CA* provides a bibliography of writings by the author, including books, chapters, and other pieces that have appeared in monographs. *CA* is available as a series of printed volumes (as of 2002 approximately 100) and as part of the Gale Literary Databases produced by the Gale Group. *CA* includes a lengthy entry on Warren Bennis, including a four-page bibliography of his writings.

Most countries and professional organizations are represented by biographical sources such as those already mentioned. For example, the American Sociological Association publishes a directory that contains much of the same information at the APA *Directory*. *Who's Who in Canada* has been published under different titles since 1912. There are many such directories, and they vary in frequency of publication and scope.

Other Biographical Sources

A variety of other biographical and autobiographical sources are available. The *History of Psychology in Autobiography* presents a series of lengthy autobiographical essays by some of the most influential American psychologists. These are especially useful for the student of psychology's history. Each essay includes the life history of the person, discussions of his or her contributions, and a selected bibliography. Among the psychologists represented are S. S. Stevens, B. F. Skinner, G. W. Allport, R. S. Woodworth, R. M. Yerkes, and L. J. Cronbach. *The Psychologists* by T. S. Krawiec (1972, 1974, 1978) provides a similar set of autobiographical essays on 35 psychologists. Each person is distinguished by his or her contributions in research, teaching, or writing. The volume includes essays on A. Anastasi, R. B. Cattell, H. Helson, W. J. McKeachie, C. E. Osgood, and R. I. Watson.

Portraits of Pioneers in Psychology, edited by Gregory A. Kimball (1991–2000) and others, is a four-volume set that provides biographical essays on individuals who influenced the early history of psychology. Each volume contains a portrait of about 20 persons. Included are notables as J. Dewey, H. Ebbinghaus, G. Fechner, L. Gilbreth, K. Spence, and B. Underwood.

Two interesting sources provide information on women psychologists. In *The Women of Psychology* Stevens and Gardner (1981–1982) provide biographies of more than 100 individuals. Although not all are psychologists by training, all made significant contributions to the field. In *Models of Achievement* O'Connell and Russo (1983–2001) offer the perspective of women on psychology.

D. L. Sills (1979) includes biographies of 215 social scientists in the *Biographical Supplement* to the *International Encyclopedia of the Social Sciences*. Sheehy, Chapman, and Conroy (1997) offered additional sketches in their *Biographical Dictionary of Psychology*.

DISSERTATIONS

Sources Discussed

Comprehensive dissertation index. (1973–present). Ann Arbor, MI: University Microfilms International. Annual. Retrospective set covers 1861–1972.

Dissertation abstracts international. Part A: Humanities and social sciences. Part B: Sciences and engineering. (1938–present). Ann Arbor, MI: University Microfilms International. Monthly. *Part C. Worldwide*. (1976–present). Ann Arbor, MI: University Microfilms International. Quarterly.

Dissertation abstracts online. Ann Arbor, MI: University Microfilms International.

As discussed in chapter 5, dissertations are the result of original research pursued as one of the requirements of a doctoral program. As such, research reported in dissertations constitutes an important body of literature in psychology. Most dissertations are unpublished and thus difficult to obtain. Dissertations are indexed in PsycINFO as well as in other indexing sources.

Universities granting doctoral degrees typically retain only a few copies of a dissertation, and these are often restricted to in-library use. Copies of most dissertations written in the United States are forwarded to University Microfilms International (UMI). On receipt of the dissertation, UMI announces its availability in *Dissertation Abstracts International (DAI)* and sells copies of dissertations in microform and paper copy formats. Each year *DAI* adds citations covering more than 50,000 dissertations. According to UMI the database contains more than 1.4 million entries and includes citations starting with the first dissertation accepted in the United States in 1861. Since 1980 dissertations in the database include the author's abstract; since 1988 abstracts of master's theses are included. *DAI* is available in hard copy, and Dissertation Abstracts Online is available electronically through an Internet subscription and in CD-ROM format. This source combines access to the *DAI* series, *Comprehensive Dissertation Index*, *Masters Abstracts International*, and *American Doctoral Dissertations*.

Recall that Warren Bennis received his doctorate in 1955 from MIT. It might be interesting to learn about his dissertation. Using Dissertation Abstracts Online through FirstSearch, we specified a search for Warren Bennis in 1955 and retrieved a record that appears like Figure 10.2. We note that the dissertation involved the study of values and institutional practices (14) and was in the field of sociology (15). Remember that dissertations in this database are not accompanied by an abstract until 1980. In this case the notice of this dissertation was published in 1955.

Given the influence that Bennis has had on the field of leadership, it might be interesting to see whether his work has influenced the work of more recent doctoral degree recipients. We then conduct a search in Dissertation Abstracts Online, specifying a Boolean search: the keywords are *leadership* **AND** *values* **AND** *Bennis*. In this case the search retrieves the occurrence of *Bennis* in the abstract as well as in the author field. Five interesting dissertations were identified by this search, including the one by Larry Wayne Cartner (16), "In Search of a Reflective Spirit," (17) shown in Figure 10.3 (p. 131). We note that this was for a Doctor of Education degree (18), granted in 1996 (19) from Peabody

Database:	Dissertations
Title:	**SOCIAL SCIENCE RESEARCH ORGANZIATION: STUDY OF THE VALUES AND INSTITUTIONAL PRACTICES IN INTERDISCIPLINARY RESEARCH**
Author(s):	BENNIS, WARREN G.
Degree:	PH.D.
Year:	1955
Pages:	00930
Institution:	MASSACHUSETTS INSTITUTE OF TECHNOLOGY; 0753
Source:	ADD, W1955, (1955): 0240
	SUBJECT(S)
Descriptor:	SOCIOLOGY, GENERAL
Accession No:	AAG0201409

(14)

(15)

FIGURE 10.2. Sample dissertation record from Dissertation Abstracts Online for Warren Bennis. From Dissertation Abstracts Online, copyright University Microfilms International. Reprinted by permission.

College for Teachers of Vanderbilt University (20), under the direction of Terrence Deal. A summary of the dissertation is provided (21). Four descriptors (22) are used to index this dissertation in the printed subject index to *DAI*. A unique identifying number for this item in the database is provided (23), which is useful if you choose to order a copy of the dissertation.

BOOK REVIEWS

Sources Discussed

Book review index. (1965–present). Detroit, MI: Gale Research.
Contemporary psychology. (1956–present). Washington, DC: American Psychological Association.
Wilson Business Database. (1995–present). New York: H. W. Wilson.

Book reviews in professional journals serve many purposes. Some faculty members consult reviews in selecting textbooks for courses. Researchers scan reviews for important new books in their field. Ideally, reviews are not limited to a description of a book's content and a statement of recommendation or censure. Reviews may be useful for their discussion of a book in the context of other literature in the field. Reviewers for scholarly journals are typically academics who are well acquainted with the body of literature of their field. They are often able to evaluate a book's contribution from the perspective of another person in the field.

Contemporary Psychology (CP) provides evaluative reviews of current psychological materials. Although its emphasis is on books of interest to psychologists and their students, films, tapes, and other media are included. Each issue of *CP* contains extensive

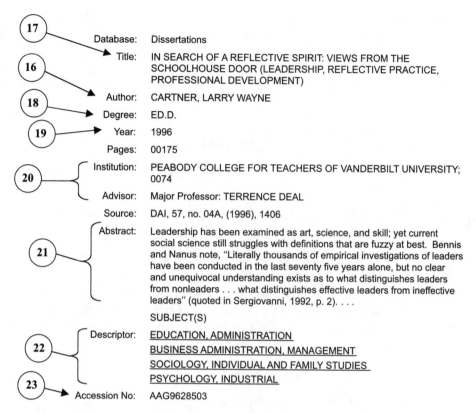

(17) Database: Dissertations

(16) Title: IN SEARCH OF A REFLECTIVE SPIRIT: VIEWS FROM THE
                   SCHOOLHOUSE DOOR (LEADERSHIP, REFLECTIVE PRACTICE,
                   PROFESSIONAL DEVELOPMENT)

(18) Author: CARTNER, LARRY WAYNE

     Degree: ED.D.

(19) Year: 1996

     Pages: 00175

(20) Institution: PEABODY COLLEGE FOR TEACHERS OF VANDERBILT UNIVERSITY;
                   0074

     Advisor: Major Professor: TERRENCE DEAL

     Source: DAI, 57, no. 04A, (1996), 1406

(21) Abstract: Leadership has been examined as art, science, and skill; yet current
                   social science still struggles with definitions that are fuzzy at best. Bennis
                   and Nanus note, "Literally thousands of empirical investigations of leaders
                   have been conducted in the last seventy five years alone, but no clear
                   and unequivocal understanding exists as to what distinguishes leaders
                   from nonleaders . . . what distinguishes effective leaders from ineffective
                   leaders" (quoted in Sergiovanni, 1992, p. 2). . . .

                   SUBJECT(S)

(22) Descriptor: EDUCATION, ADMINISTRATION
                   BUSINESS ADMINISTRATION, MANAGEMENT
                   SOCIOLOGY, INDIVIDUAL AND FAMILY STUDIES
                   PSYCHOLOGY, INDUSTRIAL

(23) Accession No: AAG9628503

FIGURE 10.3. Sample record from Dissertation Abstracts Online for a dissertation retrieved with the search leadership AND values AND Bennis using OCLC's FirstSearch. From Dissertation Abstracts Online, copyright University Microfilms International. Reprinted by permission.

reviews of approximately 20 titles, with additional books receiving briefer reviews. Books are critiqued on their merits in relation to existing psychological literature. Each December issue contains an annual index.

Unfortunately *CP* is not indexed in the PsycINFO database and citations to reviews in selected psychology journals have been added to the database only since late 2002. Thus we turn to other indexing sources to locate book reviews. Reviews appearing in *CP* are indexed in *Book Review Index* and several other sources. H. W. Wilson, in its Wilson Web (discussed in chapter 6), provides citations to book reviews in several of its index databases such as Wilson Business Index (see chapter 6). The Institute of Scientific Information's Web of Science (discussed in chapter 7) also covers book reviews in its databases.

Having learned a bit about Warren Bennis and his dissertation, let us look at how his writing has been received in the field. We seek a review of *Organizing Genius*, a book he wrote with Patricia Biederman, which focuses on great leaders and great groups. Choosing to consult Wilson Web, our search specified: *Bennis* **AND** *document type* = book review. Wilson Web returned 124 records, including reviews of *Managing People Is Like Herding Cats*; *Douglas McGregor, Revisited*; and *Beyond Leadership*. We found reviews of *Organizing Genius* in both scholarly and applied publications, including

Entrepreneur, Management Review, Organizational Dynamics, and *People Management.* Item number 20 of the 124 records represents a review (24) in *Training and Development* as shown in Figure 10.4.

  Selecting the hyperlinked title, we are able to see the bibliographic entry for this item. For many articles you will be able to select a small pictorial icon (not pictured here)

Search Results: 124 Records
Search: (bennis) and (BOOK-REVIEW in DT)

Record 18 of 124 <u>Organizing genius (book review)</u>; Sloan Management Review v 38 Spring 1997. p. 105–6

Record 19 of 124 <u>Organizing genius (book review)</u>; Across the Board v 34 Apr 1997. p. 58–9

Record 20 of 124 <u>Organizing genius (book review)</u>; Training and Development (Alexandria, Va) v 51 Apr 1997. p. 50–1

FIGURE 10.4. Subset of 124 records retrieved from Wilson Web search of Wilson Business Index for Bennis **AND** Document Type = Book Review. From *Business Periodicals Index* © 2002 The H. W. Wilson Company. All rights reserved. For more information please visit www.hwwilson.com

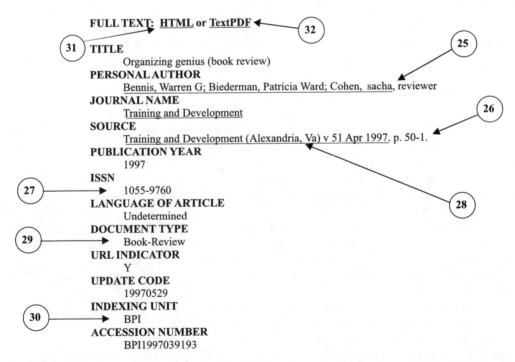

FIGURE 10.5. Sample record retrieved from Wilson Business Index using Wilson Web for a book review of *Organizing Genius.* From *Business Periodicals Index* © 2002 The H. W. Wilson Company. All rights reserved. For more information please visit www.hwwilson.com

to display page images of the article in an Adobe Acrobat PDF format or another small pictorial icon (not pictured here) to display the full text of the article.

Sacha Cohen (25) authored the review of *Organizing Genius*, illustrated in Figure 10.5 (p. 132). This review appeared on pages 50–51 in volume 51 of the April 1997 issue of the magazine *Training and Development* (26). Because there are several journals with the same title it is important to note that this is ISSN 1055-9760 (27), a journal published in Alexandria, Virginia (28). This is an item of document type = book review (29). It was selected from the *BPI* (Business) database (30). We could select HTML (31) to view a hypertext version of this article or TextPDF (32) for an Adobe Acrobat PDF image of the article.

REFERENCES

Bass, B. M. (1981). *Stogdill's handbook of leadership: A survey of theory and research* (Rev. ed.). New York: Free Press.

Bennis, W. G. (1989a). *On becoming a Leader*. Reading, MA: Addison-Wesley.

Bennis, W. G. (1989b). *Why leaders can't lead*. San Francisco, CA: Jossey-Bass.

Bennis, W. G. (1997a). *Managing people is like herding cats: The unconscious conspiracy continues*. Provo, UT: Executive Excellence Publishing.

Bennis, W. G. (1997b). *Organizing genius: The secrets of creative collaboration*. Reading, MA: Addison-Wesley.

Blake, R. R., & Mouton, J. S. (1964). *The managerial grid*. Houston, TX: Gulf.

Curtis, Q. F., Smith, R. E., & Smoll, F. L. (1979). Scrutinizing the skipper: A study of behaviors in the dugout. *Journal of Applied Psychology, 64,* 391–400.

Fiedler, F. E. (1971). *Leadership*. New York: General Learning Press.

Fleishman, E. A. (1953). The description of supervisory behavior. *Journal of Applied Psychology, 37,* 1–6.

Heio, G., Bennis, W., & Stephens, D. (2000). *Douglas McGregor, revisited: Managing the human side of the enterprise*. New York: John Wiley.

Hersey, P., & Blanchard, K. H. (1969). *Management of organizational behavior*. Englewood Cliffs, NJ: Prentice-Hall.

History of psychology in autobiography (Vols. 1–4). (1930–1952). New York: Russell & Russell.

History of psychology in autobiography (Vol. 5). (1967). New York: Appleton-Century-Crofts.

History of psychology in autobiography (Vol. 6). (1974). Englewood Cliffs, NJ: Prentice-Hall.

History of psychology in autobiography (Vol. 7). (1980). San Francisco: W. H. Freeman.

History of psychology in autobiography (Vol. 8). (1989). Stanford, CA: Stanford University Press.

Kenny, D. A., & Zaccaro, S. J. (1983). An estimate of variance due to traits in leadership. *Journal of Applied Psychology, 68,* 678–685.

Kimble, G. A., Boneau, C. A., & Wertheimer, M. (Eds.). (1996). *Portraits of pioneers in psychology* (Vol. 2). Washington, DC: American Psychological Association; Mahwah, NJ: Erlbaum.

Kimble, G. A., & Wertheimer, M. (Eds.). (1998–2000). *Portraits of pioneers in psychology* (Vols. 3–4). Washington, DC: American Psychological Association; Mahwah, NJ: Erlbaum.

Kimble, G. A., Wertheimer, M., & White, C. L. (Eds.). (1991). *Portraits of pioneers in psychology.* Washington, DC: American Psychological Association; Hillsdale, NJ: Erlbaum.

Kotter, J. (1996). *Leading change.* Cambridge, MA: Harvard Business School Press.

Kouzes, J., & Posner, B. (1995). *The leadership challenge.* San Francisco: Jossey-Bass.

Krawiec, T. S. (1972–1978). *The psychologists* (Vols. 1–3). New York: Oxford University Press.

O'Connell, A. N., & Russo, N. F. (Eds.). (1983–2001). *Models of achievement: Reflections of eminent women in psychology.* New York: Columbia University Press.

Quinn, R. E., & Spreitzer, G. M. (1997, Autumn). The road to empowerment: Seven questions every leader should consider. *Organizational Dynamics, 26*(2), 37–49.

Shartle, C. L. (1950). Leadership aspects of administrative behavior. *Advanced Management, 15,* 12–15.

Sheehy, N., Chapman, A. J., & Conroy, W. A. (Eds.). (1997). *Biographical dictionary of psychology.* New York: Routledge Reference.

Sills, D. L. (Ed.). (1979). *International encyclopedia of the social sciences: Biographical supplement.* New York: Free Press.

Stevens, G., & Gardner, S. (1981–1982). *The women of psychology* (Vols. 1–2). Cambridge, MA: Schenkman.

Stogdill, R. G. (1948). Personal factors associated with leadership: A survey of the literature. *Journal of Psychology, 25,* 35–71.

Stogdill, R. G. (1957). *Leader behavior: Its description and measurement.* Columbus, OH: Ohio State University.

11 It's Not in the Library

BY NOW you have used indexes, abstracts, and other sources to search for information. However, the library may not have all of the materials you seek. There are two major resources we have not yet discussed: use of interlibrary loan for materials not available in your library and use of the World Wide Web.

Space and finances limit library resources. Librarians must make choices when selecting materials to add to the collection—monographs, serials, and journals. Increasingly, librarians are taking advantage of electronic resources to address a shortage of space in their libraries and to take advantage of the flexibility that these tools offer their users. However, the cost of materials, whether print or electronic, dictates that not all items you need may be in your library. After exhausting your library's resources, how or where can you obtain additional materials?

INTERLIBRARY LOAN OVERVIEW AND RATIONALE

Libraries willing to assist one another in meeting the information needs of their users belong to one or more library networks. Within these networks, they engage in reciprocal borrowing and lending activities. Thus, a library may be able to obtain for one of its users a copy of a journal article, a book, a government publication, or some other material from another library. Through these networks, using a service known as interlibrary loan (ILL), you may have access to collections of materials located in other cities or states.

ILL policies vary among libraries and networks. Each library establishes its own guidelines based on local funding, staffing, and other priorities. An ILL librarian or reference librarian can inform you about your library's policies and procedures. If you decide you would like to use ILL, you need to keep several points in mind.

First, ILL takes more time than locating items owned locally. Although many libraries now obtain articles electronically from other institutions, requested hard-copy materials seldom arrive in less than a week. A rare journal or book owned by only a few libraries (as may be the case for materials published in other countries or by small publishing houses) may involve lengthier waits. Thus, you must begin your search early. Allow time to compile a list of references, check your library's collection, and request materials through ILL. Once you do receive the materials you will need time to read and analyze them before you write your report.

Second, ILL procedures differ from library to library. Some libraries provide this service only to faculty members, others to faculty and graduate students, still others to all members of the academic community. Therefore, you must inquire about whether ILL is available to you.

Third, you must provide complete bibliographic information for the materials you wish to obtain. Doing so is not a problem if you have consistently and accurately noted all of the information you have found in an indexing or abstracting service. If you have not kept complete records, you will need to retrace search steps to fill in bibliographic gaps.

Fourth, some libraries charge for ILL service, especially to satisfy journal article requests. Libraries seldom lend an entire issue or volume of a journal. Instead, the article you request will be photocopied and sent to your library. The cost of photocopying and a service charge may be passed on to you. In addition, libraries do not loan some types of materials. These include reference materials (such as encyclopedias and biographical directories), tests, and rare and manuscript material.

Fifth, this is a library-to-library service. You must work through your ILL librarian to request and receive materials. You cannot directly request materials from another library.

INTERLIBRARY LOAN PROCESS

After you verify that you are eligible to use ILL services, decide what materials you really need to request. Given the time delay involved and potential charges, you need to identify what is essential for your project and separate these materials from the nonessential (tangential, trivial, or redundant) materials. Reviewing information contained in the abstracts of articles retrieved through searches discussed earlier in this book may help you evaluate the potential relevance of materials.

Once you have determined what you need, you must complete an ILL request form for each item you want. As with many other services the procedures vary from library to library. Some libraries require use of paper forms, whereas others allow you to submit requests electronically using e-mail or forms on the library's Web site. Consult someone on your library's reference staff for information specific to your library. Whatever the procedure, keep a record of the materials you request. Such records prevent you from making duplicate requests, save you time, and let you know what to expect.

We cannot stress too highly the importance of complete and accurate information in your ILL request. If you do not provide complete and accurate information, several things may happen. Your library may reject your request because your information is inadequate for locating the materials you have requested. If your information is inaccurate you may not get what you were expecting. If your information is inaccurate or incomplete it may take extra time to identify and locate the material you have requested.

When requesting a journal article, you can help the process. Because ILL staff members handle so many incomplete requests, they often ask for the source of the citation. Our experience is that many librarians are more comfortable about the accuracy of a journal article request if they can actually see the citation as it appeared in the indexing or abstracting service. If you found the article in PsycINFO, Educational Resources Information Center (ERIC), *Sociological Abstracts,* or some other database, make a photocopy of the entry and attach it to your ILL request form, or include the database name and a citation number if you submit your request electronically. Because there are many similar and identical journal titles, include the International Standard Serial Number (ISSN) if it is provided. This can increase the likelihood of getting the right article. If you are working from a list of references in a book, review, or handbook rather than from an index or abstract, include bibliographic information about the book and the page number where you found the citation. If the reference looks suspicious (that is, missing the year of publication or page numbers) and it is a key reference for your paper, try to verify the citation in a standard source such as PsycINFO (see chapter 5) or ERIC (see chapter 6).

When requesting a book through ILL, accuracy of your citation is equally important. Many millions of books have been published. Books may have very similar titles by authors with very similar names and can be published in multiple editions. As with a journal, the book request form may ask you for the source of the citation, so be accurate. If available, include information such as the International Standard Book Number (ISBN), which uniquely identifies the title you need, and if you need a specific edition. If you have questions you might choose to validate the citation for your book by using an online catalog to find it, such as the Library of Congress (LC) online catalog, the Online Computer Library Catalog (OCLC), or a statewide catalog of holdings such as Wisconsin's WISCAT (see chapter 4).

When you submit your ILL request, inquire about notification procedures. Will the library send an article to you electronically or send e-mail when your materials arrive? Must you contact the library? When might you anticipate receipt of materials? Make sure you understand any billing procedures.

Why does ILL consume so much time, even if your request is submitted electronically? Your request takes many steps. In the case of a journal article ILL request, a staff member at your (requesting) library may have to verify your information (especially if it is incomplete, uses many abbreviations, has no citation source, has a citation source that is not a bibliographic database, or looks unusual). The librarian next locates information about the item from a standard bibliographic source and identifies a library that owns the requested journal and can supply it before your deadline. The request is then made by your library. Staff in the responding library locate the material requested, make a copy of it, detail any charges and prepare a bill, and send the material to your library. Once the material is received, someone contacts you. Each step in the process takes time. Delays and problems of many types may occur. If you have provided incomplete or inaccurate information, your request may wait for verification while others are processed. The librarian may have difficulty locating a rare or obscure source. The article you need may be missing from the responding library. A bibliographic source indicating that a library has the material you seek may be in error, in which case the library must notify your requesting library. A holiday, absent staff member, or inoperable copying machine may delay the process. Occasionally, someone makes an error. In spite of these potential problems, however, in time ILL can generally provide the information you need.

TRAVEL TO OTHER LIBRARIES

In some circumstances you may want to travel to a neighboring library to use materials. Before you go, determine if your library and the library you plan to visit are members of a college or university library consortium or network. If there is a special network user ID card, ask if you are eligible for one. Such cooperative arrangements among libraries sometimes include borrowing privileges for students affiliated with member institutions, access to reference services or special collections, or use of specialized indexes or reference materials your home library does not own. If the library you plan to visit has a catalog on the Internet, you can search the catalog to verify that it owns the material you need before you make the trip.

A few cautions are in order. In visiting the libraries of other colleges or universities, you are their guest. They may have rules that limit your access to materials or do not permit you to use all of their resources. For example, the library may not loan materials to you directly or may not permit use of some electronic resources.

ELECTRONIC RESOURCES: WORLD WIDE WEB

In the past 10 years a host of electronic information resources has become available, typically in the form of Web sites on the Internet. Why might you want to consult information on the Web? According to Arnold and Jayne (1998) the Internet offers several strengths as a source of information. One, online information can be very current; the delay from the time when the information becomes available and when you get it can be very brief. Two, uniqueness; some information on the Internet is not available elsewhere. Three, availability; access to information on the Internet is not limited by time or space (although this does not mean information is not copyrighted in the same way that traditional printed materials are). Additionally, as Branch, Kim, and Koenecke (1999) noted, the Internet offers a very inexpensive means of distributing information worldwide. There are many types of sources of information on the Internet.

Professional Organizations

Many professional organizations, such as the American Psychological Association (APA), American Psychological Society (APS), National Mental Health Association (NMHA), and the Psychonomic Society maintain Web sites. These sites make available a great deal of information on psychology for members as well as for others interested in the field. They provide links to publications, press releases, data about the organization and membership, and convention information. Many organizations segment their information on Web sites into that which is available to anyone, available only to members or subscribers, or available via an intranet accessible only to the employees of the organization. For example, the APS Web site at http://www.psychologicalscience.org provides two types of access. It allows anyone accessing the site to view employment advertisements, activities of its student caucus, and events planned for its annual convention. However, you must have a member password to access the APS Member Directory and the complete contents of its journal publications, *Psychological Science* and *Current Directions in Psychological Science*.

Electronic Publications

A second resource is online publications. They may duplicate their printed counterparts in their entirety, may include just excerpts or selected articles from an issue, or may exist only in an electronic format. Electronic resources can be one of two types.

Freely Available

Generally, these are newsletters such as the APS *Observer* and the APA *Monitor on Psychology*, which publish at least part of their printed publications on a Web site. Another example is the experimental journal, *Psycoloquy*, an interdisciplinary, refereed publication covering all areas of psychology. *Classics in the History of Psychology* (http://psychclassics.yorku.ca/topic.htm) features electronic versions of classic books and articles from the early years of psychology. Works of Binet, Dewey, Galton, James, Münsterberg, Titchener, Watson, Yerkes, and others are included.

Subscription-Based

Although individuals can subscribe to services that permit them to read the complete text of publications online, most subscribers to these services are libraries. For example, Annual Reviews, Inc., publisher of *Annual Reviews of Psychology* and similar volumes covering other disciplines (http://www.annualreviews.org), provides access to its publications online. Many publishers that produce books and journals in many disciplines (such as Cambridge University Press and Academic Press) make their publications available in this way. Elsevier Science, for instance, publishes both printed and electronic versions of its journals *Addictive Behaviors*, *Cognitive Development*, and *Intelligence*.

Web Links

Other sites are collection points that provide online links to Web sites containing information believed to be useful. One of the older, more established Web sites in psychology is *Dr. John Grohol's Psych Central* (http://www.psychcentral.com/). Included here are articles, self-quizzes, access to discussion forums, book reviews, and more. Other interesting and potentially useful sites are Psych Web, Internet Mental Health, Psychology Online Resource Central, and the Psychology Virtual Library. Many college libraries and psychology departments maintain similar sites.

Other Sites

There are many other types of sites on the Web. Some sites are created by a service or product provider such as a consulting firm, publisher, or psychologist. Some exist because someone has information he or she wants to make available. Others exist just because someone wants to have a Web site ("vanity" site). Promotional and e-commerce sites are available to advertise or promote a product or service. Other sites advocate a particular political or social cause (Tillman, 1995). Methods for evaluating the usefulness of all these sites are covered later in this chapter.

Search Engines

Suppose you think there might be some information on the Internet that will help you, but you are not sure where it is located. You can use a search engine to locate specific information on the Internet. There are several search engines available. On the surface they appear pretty similar, but the way they operate and the results they produce differ significantly.

Directories

A directory, such as Yahoo! (http://www.yahoo.com), is constructed by directory editors. Web site managers submit a description of their site to directory editors, or the editors may develop a description of a site. Sites the directory editors choose to include are added to the directory database, with information about them organized in categories and subcategories. The effect is like building a library subject catalog. When you search the directory site, the directory displays a list of sites that match your request. Other popular directory-based search engines are About.com, LookSmart, and Open Directory (Goldsborough, 2000, 2001; London, 2000; Norton, 2001; Sullivan, 2001). Some of the most established directories were begun by libraries, including the Internet Public Library (http://www.ipl.org/), which began in 1995 at the University of Michigan.

Crawlers/Spiders

A search engine lets you search for information in an electronically created database. A search engine such as AltaVista (http://www.altavista.com) sends out automated "spiders" that "crawl" through the Internet, gathering information from words on Web pages and then indexing that information in a database. When you use these search engines by using subject terms, the search is conducted in the index it has compiled. The result is a list of Web pages that, based on the indexing database, match your request. One of the most popular search engines of 2001 was Google. Other popular spider-type search engines include Fast, Lycos, Northern Light, and WebCrawler (Goldsborough, 2000, 2001; Gowan & Spanbauer, 2001; London, 2000; Norton, 2001; Sullivan, 2001). Some engines, such as Google, use a spider to locate information and also provide users with a directory-type organization of information.

Metasearch Engines

Metasearch engines comprise a slightly different class. These engines do not maintain their own database or catalog. Instead, when users make a request, the metasearch engine queries other search engines such as those just described. Metasearch engines provide results of the combined search to the user in some type of organized form (Kent, 2001; Norton, 2001). Results may be organized by frequency of "hit" or relevance to the search terms you used, based on a weighting algorithm. Some metasearch engines may allow the user to select which search engines to query. Among the most popular metasearch engines are Dogpile, HotBot, and MetaCrawler (Garman, 1999; Gowan & Spanbauer, 2001).

Search engines differ in the conventions they use. Many allow Boolean searching and text strings or phrases, some offer very simple search queries, and others allow construction of more complex search statements. Some sites permit both. The Internet is constantly changing; with millions of sites available on the World Wide Web, some sites available today may be gone tomorrow, and new ones appear every day. New search engines are developed (e.g., ProFusion), and others disappear (e.g., Magellan); one company merges with another (e.g., Lycos and HotBot); and the databases that support these sites are constantly updated as spiders collect information on Web pages and editors add sites. Because of these and other factors, the results you obtain from one search may differ from the same search you conduct on that same site or on another site just a few days later. Notess (1999) offered several cautions and suggestions when using Internet search engines. First, be flexible and apply critical analysis to all search results. Second, never completely trust the results from a search engine; that is, do not expect unfailing consistency or accuracy. Some engines do not search their entire database, do not cover the entire Web, and may not report some sites when a portion of the database is offline. Third, analyze results, identify discrepancies, and modify your search as you go.

To find out more about search engines, refer to *Guides to Specialized Search Engines*, developed and maintained by Paula Dragutsky (1999). Available via http://www.searchability.com, this is a list of dozens of guides to search engines with a description of what each attempts to accomplish. Another interesting site is Search Engine Watch, developed and maintained by Sullivan and Sherman (2002). Available at http://searchenginewatch.com, it provides a variety of tips and information about searching and search engines.

How should you proceed? Find a good search engine. If you are not sure which one to use, consult a current issue of a magazine such as *Online* or an article such as that by Gowan and Spanbauer (2001), or ask a librarian. Find out about the search engine you select. What type is it? How does it operate? Test it to see how it behaves; for example, define a search, conduct the search in a variety of ways, and compare the results. Monitor the success of your searches, and occasionally use an alternative search engine for comparison.

Invisible Web

Much of what we have discussed in earlier chapters of this book is a part of what some authors have referred to as the invisible Web (Dahn, 2000; Smith 2001). This refers to information that cannot be retrieved by an Internet search engine. Examples include databases that require a log-in, sites that require a fee for use, sites that allow only their own search software to query the database, and sites on a private or internal network behind a firewall (e.g., a company intranet Web site). Many of the library resources discussed elsewhere in this book are part of this invisible Web, for example, PsycINFO, PubMed, ERIC, MEDLINE. Thus, to be thorough you must conduct multiple searches using different databases. The Internet search must be an addition to your search of the library's resources and not be a replacement for it.

Caution in Using Resources on the World Wide Web

Although the World Wide Web can be a great source of information, many cautions are in order. Most important is the concern about the quality of the information you retrieve. Articles contained in refereed journals (e.g., *American Psychologist, Psychonomic Society Bulletin*) have been through a peer review process (see chapter 5). As a result of the review process, articles with significant errors, unfounded claims, or inadequate data tend to be rejected and are not published. Much information placed on the Web is not submitted to a formal review process before it appears. As a result you must exercise care in reviewing, evaluating, and using the data you retrieve.

Beck (1997), Kirk (1996), Skov (1998), Tate and Alexander (1996), and others have offered guidelines for evaluating online information and Web sites. Five general criteria have been proposed, similar to criteria used for evaluating works published in print format. These criteria, which you should consider, follow.

Authority

Who is responsible for the information, and is the source reliable? Is the author of the site clearly identified? Are the qualifications of this person to write on this topic available? Is this a reputable, legitimate author on this topic?

Accuracy

Is the information on the Web site accurate, and can you verify it? Are verifiable sources of information contained on the site provided in the form of a bibliography or reference list? If the site offers research results, is the methodology used to gather and analyze the data clearly identified and appropriate? Are theories, techniques, and sources described and used appropriately? Is the source relatively error-free and well written, indicating that care has been taken in its preparation?

Objectivity

Is the information offered as a public service and relatively free from bias? Does the site appear to be relatively free of political or philosophical bias, or is there a clear agenda? Is there advertising on the site? Is the information contained on the site subject to any type of a review process? Is the site sponsored by a particular organization, and does that organization have a bias or particular agenda?

Currency

Is the site still available? When was the information written? When was it last updated?

Coverage

What topics does this site cover? Is there a print equivalent of this information, and is it the same as on the site? What information does this site offer that is unavailable elsewhere? How much depth is provided?

Beck (1997) characterized Web sites as good, bad, and ugly. Just as a basic principal in commerce is *caveat emptor* (buyer beware), keep a similar caveat in mind when using Internet information; that is, user beware. There are good Web sites and bad Web sites. Some sites contain reliable, valid, accurate, useful information; others do not. Your challenge is to sort out the good from the bad. Use the preceding criteria to evaluate information you retrieve.

Happy searching!

REFERENCES

Arnold, J. M., & Jayne, E. A. (1998). Dangling by a slender thread: The lessons and implications of teaching the World Wide Web to freshmen. *Journal of Academic Librarianship, 24*, 43–52.

Beck, S. (1997). *The good, the bad, & the ugly: Or, why it's a good idea to evaluate web sources.* Retrieved December 31, 2001, from http://lib.nmsu.edu/instruction/evalcrit.html

Branch, R. M., Kim, D., & Koenecke, L. (1999, June). Evaluating online educational materials for use in instruction. *ERIC Digest* [Microfiche]. Syracuse, NY: ERIC Clearinghouse on Information and Technology. (ERIC Document Reproduction Service No. ED430564.)

Dahn, M. (2000, July/August). Spotlight on the invisible web. *Online, 24*(4), 57–62. Retrieved January 11, 2002, from Academic Search Elite (AN 3290452).

Dragutsky, P. (1999). *Guides to specialized search engines.* Retrieved January 11, 2002, from http://www.searchability.com/ Updated October 1, 2001.

Garman, N. (1999, May/June). Meta search engines. *Online, 23*(3), 74–78. Retrieved January 7, 2002, from Academic Search Elite (AN 1801191).

Goldsborough, R. (2000, December). New internet search options. *Consumers' Research Magazine, 83*(12), 32. Retrieved January 11, 2002, from Academic Search Elite (AN 3918764).

Goldsborough, R. (2001, June). Searching for the best web sites around . . . or for whatever you need. *Poptronics, 2*(6), 21–24. Retrieved January 11, 2002, from Academic Search Elite (AN 4444387).

Gowan, M., & Spanbauer, S. (2001, September). Find everything faster. *PC World, 19*(9), 109–115. Retrieved January 11, 2002, from Academic Search Elite (AN 4958888).

Kent, M. L. (2001, Spring). Essential tips for searching the web. *Public Relations Quarterly, 46*(1), 26–30.

Kirk, E. E. (1996). *Evaluating information found on the Internet.* Retrieved February 3, 2002, from http://www.library.jhu.edu/elp/useit/evaluate/index.html Updated July 16, 2001.

London, D. (2000, August 14). Solving the search riddle. *B to B, 85*(12), 20–21. Retrieved January 11, 2002, from Business Source Elite (AN 3481542).

Norton, P. (2001) *Introduction to computers* (4th ed.). New York: Glencoe/McGraw-Hill.

Notess, G. R. (1999, September/October). On-the-fly search engine analysis. *Online, 23*(5), 63–64, 66. Retrieved January 11, 2002, from Academic Search Elite (AN 2192266).

Skov, A. (1998, August/September). Separating the wheat from the chaff: Internet quality. *Database, 21*(4), 38–40. Retrieved January 3, 2002, from Academic Search Elite (AN 908428).

Smith, C. B. (2001, Summer). Getting to know the invisible web. *Library Journal, 126*(11), 16–18.

Sullivan, D. (2001). *How search engines work.* Retrieved January 6, 2002, from http://Searchenginewatch.com/webmasters/work.html

Sullivan, D., & Sherman, C. (2002). *Search engine watch: Tips about Internet search engines and search engine submission.* Retrieved January 6, 2002, from http://searchenginewatch.com

Tate, M., & Alexander, J. (1996, November/December). Teaching critical evaluation skills for World Wide Web resources. *Computers in Libraries, 16*(10), 49–55. Retrieved January 3, 2002 from Academic Search Elite (AN 9611227689).

Tillman, H. N. (2001) *Evaluating quality on the net.* Retrieved January 2, 2002, from http://www.hopetillman.com/findqual.html Updated March 19, 2001.

Appendix:
Brief Guide to
Literature Searching

THE FOLLOWING step-by-step guidelines may help you organize and conduct your literature search. Complete each step in sequential order. As you proceed, record citations for each source located and consulted in your search. The chapters in which particular steps in the process and bibliographic resources are discussed are indicated for each step. This is not intended as a replacement for reading the book; rather, it is an outline of some of the key steps to be used.

STAGE 1: DEFINING AND LIMITING THE TOPIC (CHAPTER 2)

- State the general topic.
- Briefly define the topic.
- Identify one or two initial sources—a textbook, handbook, or article.
- Find and read a review source for general background:
  Textbook
  Annual review
  Handbook
  Review article
- Narrow your topic by one or more of the following:
  Subarea
  Theory
  Population (e.g., species, gender, age)
  Research methodology (e.g., laboratory study, case study, naturalistic observation)
  Time period
- Restate the narrowed topic statement or research question.
- Consider: Is there further need to narrow the topic? How?
- Ask self-analyzing questions:
  What do I find most interesting about this topic?
  Why am I interested in this topic?
- State the narrowed topic.
- List the primary sources you have consulted.
- List the subject search terms.

STAGE 2: STRUCTURING A SEARCH (CHAPTERS 2 AND 3)

- Identify the major concepts to be included.
- Develop a list of search terms to be used for each major concept.
- Define the search structure.

STAGE 3: IDENTIFYING BIBLIOGRAPHIC RESOURCES (ENTIRE BOOK)

- Consider what types of sources for your topic you might need to locate—books, articles in psychology, articles in other disciplines, government documents, tests, research reports, and dissertations.
- Consider the types of searches you will need to conduct, for example, keyword/subject, author, and citation.
- Identify which bibliographic resources you might need to consult to find relevant citations. Develop a list of those resources, such as PsycINFO, ERIC, MEDLINE, SSCI, and government publications.

STAGE 4: FINDING BOOKS (CHAPTER 4)

Do the following for a general overview of your topic:

- List important books (if you know any) and authors (researchers in the field) you may want to investigate.
- Conduct a subject/keyword search and author search of your library catalog.

STAGE 5: FINDING JOURNAL ARTICLES— AUTHOR/SUBJECT/KEYWORD SEARCH (CHAPTERS 5 AND 6)

- Consult the bibliographic resources listed in Stage 3. For example:

  Psychology—PsycINFO

  Education—ERIC or Education Database

  Business—Business Source Elite, ABI/Inform, or Lexis-Nexis

  Health—MEDLINE

  Sociology—*Sociological Abstracts*

  Others

- Before you begin your search of a bibliographic resource, especially if you have not used it before, review a tutorial on how to use the service and notes about unique features of the resource.
- Before you begin your search of a bibliographic resource, consult the thesaurus to validate your subject search terms for that service.

STAGE 6: CITATION SEARCH CONSIDERATION (CHAPTER 7)

Answer the following questions:

- Do I have access to SSCI or another citation searching service (e.g., PsycINFO)? Does the search service cover the desired time period?
- Do I have an important early citation on my topic critical to development in this area that everyone probably references?

If you answer "yes" to these you may wish to consider a citation search. If you answer "no" to any one of these, then a citation search is not on your list.

STAGE 7: LOCATING GOVERNMENT DOCUMENTS (CHAPTER 8)

Is this topic an area in which government agencies have a strong interest, such as mental health, aging, or disabilities? If "yes," then you may find government documents useful.

- Consult GPO Access.

STAGE 8: FINDING A MEASURE (CHAPTER 9)

If you are planning to do an empirical study, do you need to use some type of a measure (test) to gather data? Are there particular tests or measures referred to in the research you are reading?

- Consult a source on tests and measures, such as *MMY*.

STAGE 9: FINDING BIOGRAPHIC OR OTHER INFORMATION (CHAPTER 10)

Do you need information about a person rather than a topic?

- Consult a biographical resource.

STAGE 10: IS EVERYTHING AVAILABLE IN YOUR LIBRARY? (CHAPTER 11)

Consider interlibrary loan, but before you do, ask yourself the following:

- Is interlibrary loan service available to me?
- Is there no charge or a charge that I can afford for interlibrary loan?
- How long will interlibrary loan take? Will I have information in time?
- Do I really need the materials not in my library?

If you answer "yes" to these, then make your interlibrary loan requests. Consider the World Wide Web.

- Might there be other information I have not located yet?
- Evaluate the quality of information retrieved from the Internet (www).

Index

About the Authors

Jeffrey G. Reed is director of the Management Program in Business Administration at Marian College of Fond du Lac in Wisconsin, where he has taught courses in management, leadership, human resources, organizational behavior, project management, and statistics. He also taught psychology courses as a faculty member in psychology at SUNY–Geneseo and SUNY–Brockport. For 13 years at Xerox Corporation, he held positions as program/project manager, user interface design manager, and software developer. Reed has also been an organizational consultant in Rochester, New York; a reference librarian at Bucknell University; and an educational researcher at Towson University and Kansas State University. He has conducted research on motivation, satisfaction, academic performance, teaching effectiveness, human–computer interaction, and library use, and his articles have appeared in journals such as *Educational Psychology*, *Teaching of Psychology*, and *Research in Higher Education*. Reed received his PhD in psychology from Kansas State University, MA in psychology from Towson State University, MLS in library and information science from the University of Maryland, and BA in political science from Muskingum College.

Pam M. Baxter is a data archivist at the Cornell Institute for Social and Economic Research. She has held positions as lecturer in the School of Information Science and Policy at SUNY–Albany, head of the psychological sciences library at Purdue University, reference librarian at SUNY–Geneseo, and project bibliographer for the New York State Department of Education. She has written on bibliographic instruction with emphasis on the information gathering skills and literature search methods used by students and researchers in psychology and the social sciences. She is author of *Psychology: A Guide to Reference and Information Sources* (1993) and editor of *Social Science Reference Services* (1995). Pam received her MLS and BA (history) from the State University of New York at Albany.